The Mastery of Awareness Part I

Seeing Through the Eyes of the Jaguar

Kristopher Raphael

Graphic Design by:

Kalyn Raphael

Lightwurks Publishing

LightWurks LLC Publishing

Colorado Springs, Colorado

DEDICATION

I would like to express my gratitude to those Unseen Friends that assisted me in the total transformation of my life, and to Cherryl Taylor who brought Them to my awareness.

I also wish to thank all of those I have been blessed to work with, my apprentices and students who shared energy with me, enabling me to extend what I have been given.

My thanks go out to my family and their support, and to my wonderful daughter Erika for opening my heart to love.

Last but not least, I want to give my appreciation to my beautiful wife Kalyn, who showed me what it is like to truly extend and receive love, without whose dedicated assistance, this book would have been a long time coming into fruition.

Table of Contents

Prologue

The Caretakers of Humanity convened as the Earth Life System began its orbit back towards the One. "It is time to bring the hereto esoteric Schools of Direct Knowledge down into the density of mass consciousness," was the consensus.

One such School of Direct Knowledge was referred to as the Toltec Path. Until this time, Toltecs (the word Toltec means man or woman of knowledge), studied in societies hidden from the common man. The Toltec knowledge was hidden in the ethers. Now, for the first time, it was available to be accessed by anyone ready to use it. It would be transmitted through those who are capable of accessing Silent Knowledge.

It is a new paradigm, no longer will it suffice to use spirituality to go up to Spirit. Now, the true spiritual warrior must bring that spirituality back down into daily life, to make spirituality work in the Dream of the Planet.

Introduction

The Mastery of Awareness

Welcome to the Mastery of Awareness course, Part I. Learning by example is one of the quickest ways of learning. This book contains lessons given in actual Mastery of Awareness classes that took place over a twoyear period. People from various parts of the world participated in the classes. In addition to the lessons given in the classes, you will read the actual questions that students had as they worked their way through their transformation. Some of the students were just beginning their journey; others had been walking on this path for some time. Each time a class came together, a powerful collective of people with common Intent for personal growth, transformation and evolution was created. Spirit is able to work powerfully through collective groups of people. It was the *combination* of the material given, and the collective energy of the group that gave the members of the classes the opportunity for rapid transformation and growth. Many of the participants are still active in collective groups.

You as the reader can also tap into the energy that was set up through these classes. As you read the lessons, apply them. It is the application of the knowledge that gives transformation. If not applied, the knowledge given here will only add to your inventory of previous knowledge and not serve you. As you read the questions and answers, open to the energy of the person doing the questioning. Get involved in what you are reading as if you were an actual participant in the class. The more you are able to open to the feeling sensation of the question and answers, the more you will tap into the energy of the powerful collective that has been set up through these classes. Get involved with what you read. Most lessons are followed by exercises. Do the exercises. It is always tempting to skim through and take in as much information as we can. However, unless the knowledge is applied, it loses its power to invoke transformation. Once the power in the knowledge is lost, it just becomes a part of what Toltecs call our inventory. It is our inventory that stops us from perceiving the "what is" that exists just behind the veil.

So much of our lives contain a great deal of motion – we read this, we try that – much motion, but little movement. Our Intent here is to create movement in our lives in the most efficient and elegant form possible. By connecting to the energy here and applying the knowledge given, you will experience selftransformation movement in your life.

As you read the material and apply it, you may experience changes in your life, both in your innerworld (your thoughts, feelings, dreams and desires) and in your outerworld (relationships, family, living space, friends, and work). Remember, personal growth is change. While change can sometimes bring up fear or discomfort, you need to try not to resist it. Resistance only drains your energy and slows down your growth.

In addition, as you progress you may experience "stuff" come up. Emotional cleansing is a natural result of bringing in higher frequencies of energy. You may find patterns come up from your subconscious that you were not fully aware that you had. Always keep in mind that this is part of the process of cleaning, clearing and healing the human Tonal. A clean, clear, healed and strong Tonal is necessary for you to experience the Nagual (the Tonal and the Nagual will be discussed later in the book).

You want to move into creating what the Toltecs call, "the dream of heaven". This requires you to raise the frequency of your habitual platform of being. Emotional wounds and charges vibrate at a dense level, and prevent you from creating this dream.

So know that if fear, emotional discomfort or irritability comes up, it too will pass. It is just part of the clearing process.

In this book, you will read references to "unseen friends" in some of the discussions. When a collective of people with common intent is formed, it attracts much help from other planes of existence. I refer to this help as unseen friends. As the online courses progressed, many participants were able to perceive the workings of these unseen friends. The best way for you, the reader, to receive this help is for you to get involved with what you read. As you put your energy towards working the lessons and exercises, you become a part of a larger collective. This unseen help works most powerfully through a collective. This is because humans are part of a larger whole. While we are given a sense of being individual, as this helps us work out our piece of the bigger pie, we are all connected as we are working for a common purpose. It is much easier for unseen friends to work on the level of the collective than it is for them to work on the level of the individual.

So, get involved in this book. As you do, you will connect to something bigger that will assist you on your path to freedom. It is my wish that everyone who takes part in these teachings experience more freedom and joy in every step they take in life. Life is a gift, a wonderful gift. I realize that in the beginning, there is often pain, and it is difficult to make life work the way we would like it to. Nevertheless, I can tell you from experience that this is only a phase of the path and it is possible to move through this phase. As we do, we move from pain being our motivation for our spiritual path to love being our motivation. Then, each new day of our lives we awake with exquisite anticipation of the gifts life will bring us that day.

Welcome to the journey.

Love and Light,

Kristopher

Chapter 1 - Awareness

Lesson I - **The Mastery of Awareness**

Depending on the particular Toltec lineage, there are three basic Toltec Masteries – the Mastery of Awareness, the Mastery of Transformation and the Mastery of Intent. This course deals with the first Mastery, the Mastery of Awareness.

In the Mastery of Awareness, we focus on two things – freeing and heightening our awareness. In this course, we will be working on both these fronts.

Why do we start with Awareness? G. Gurdjieff, a powerful sage with his roots in Sufism, would often tell his students, "Unless a man knows he is in jail, he will never try to escape." The Toltecs call this jail the "dream of the planet", or the human form. Toltecs discovered that everything we think we know has come from this dream, and the dream is not real. They discovered the knowledge we hold so dearly prevents us from perceiving who we are. Some schools of knowledge call this our true Self. Toltecs further discovered that the only way to free up our perception so we can perceive our true Self, and what they refer to as the Nagual, is to dismantle all our beliefs, concepts, and convictions. We need to silence the mental body of its incessant chatter, called the inner dialog. In addition, we need to heal the emotional wounding that causes the emotional charges that blind us from perceiving reality as it truly is.

The Toltecs refer to our knowledge, beliefs and concepts as our inventory. The average human is only aware of a portion of their inventory, and most of their emotional wounding lies beyond their awareness, deep in their subconscious. To perceive the world of energy, our true Self, and the Nagual, we must clean, clear, heal and strengthen our Tonal. However, before we can do this we must be aware of what it is we need to clean, clear, heal and strengthen. We must increase the depth of our Awareness. The process of increasing the depth of our Awareness also frees up more Awareness, and strengthens it.

We want to get to the point where we perceive who we are, and perceive the realm of energy referred to as the second attention. With the awareness of who we are, and the ability to perceive essences and energy before they manifest in physicality, we are able to move from the dream of the planet to create our own dream of heaven. We are able to manifest powerfully our spiritual side in our daily life.

Exercise I - The Book of Life

During this course, we will be maintaining two journals: the Mitote Book, and the Book of Life. This exercise concerns the Book of Life. First, some background:

You are the dreamed, dreamed by the Dreamer; your life is the dream.

We will delve further into the dream, the dreamed and the Dreamer later in the course. However, for now we can look at the Dreamer as a higher, much larger aspect of Self. The Dreamer holds our destiny, our purpose for this lifetime, and the tools we need for spiritual evolution.

How does the Dreamer communicate with us? When we embark on the third Mastery, the Mastery of Intent, we begin to connect consciously with the Dreamer. However, until we reach the point to where we are able to do so, the Dreamer can and does communicate with us. It does so through our deep desires or urges.

Do you have a desire for personal growth? Obviously, the answer is yes. That is why you are here taking this course. Where do these desires come from? Were they something that was taught to you (religious beliefs are often taught to us), or are they something that comes from deep inside you?

Spend quiet time focusing on your desire for personal growth and transformation. Ask yourself the following questions and write down the answers in your Book of Life:

When was the first time you remember having these desires? How old were you?

How many times have they come up in your life? Sometimes, when we recall our desires we find that they have come to the surface at different times in our life. Then they fade into our depth for a while, only to appear later in life.

When these desires came up, what did you do? Sometimes, for example, if they come up early in our life, we will turn to religions or other faith and belief systems to try to find answers.

What are you doing now in accordance to these desires? Do you read books? Attend classes? What are your desires motivating you to do now in your life?

Spend the next few days focusing on your desires. Focus on what is motivating you to take this course and other personal growth and spiritual pursuits. Write down your observations in your Book of Life.

Focusing and recalling our desires for personal growth and transformation have a wonderful side affect. The more we do so, the more we connect to the Dreamer, that larger part of Self. As we do this, the Dreamer begins to make itself known in our life, eventually cocreating our life through us. By focusing on our urges, we speed up our transformation.

Spend some quiet time doing this exercise. Focus on your desires for growth so you can easily recall them as you go about your day. Then periodically during the day, whether at work or at home, recall your desires and try to *feel* them deeply. This exercise enhances your awareness. Moreover, doing this consistently will begin to bring the divine aspects of Self into your daily life.

Desire to Become Enlightened

Question: The most curious thing in my childhood was a sensation when I suddenly felt that I was standing behind myself. I mean the adult me was visiting the child me. I could not sort out that experience. That it was the adult me was only my first interpretation of it. I bring this up because I would like to know what I sensed. Was it a 'trick' by, or an effect of, the Dreamer? I felt a presence and I got a bit disturbed about it, since there was a grave message connected with it that made me uneasy. I have never told anyone that this happened, but from then on, I knew that it was something different with me.

In some way, I guess it was these early experiences of these serious eyes looking at me that made me 'know' that I had to become a searcher in some way; I had to find out how this was possible. No matter what should happen, I would only have one direction to go. I was not happy about that 'realization', and I did not give it much thought until several years later. At about 15, I became interested in eastern religions, UFOs and the paranormal, and I started to meditate.

At the age of 17, when I was in my Zenperiod, I made a decision to find enlightenment or become a shaman (!). I was a bit naïve, but was serious about doing this... I was ready to sacrifice, and let my own wealth and career step back for my spiritual development. I wanted to be a tool for Spirit. My goal for spiritual connection has changed along the way, but the original intent since my teenage years is still within me.

Answer: Thank you for sharing that. It is important that you have identified the desire for growth that you had when you were 17. Spend the next few weeks recalling it often, and focusing your awareness on it. This will speed up your process and connection.

These desires are connected to a larger aspect of you. By keeping your awareness on this desire, it will grow and the connection will amplify.

Some have these urges that come up when we are young, then leave, and then come back again. Others find themselves having a strong desire come up for the first time, later in life. Recalling the desire will begin to move you back onto the growth path, you were meant to follow when coming into body.

Having our future Self come visit us when we are children does happen, and it is more common than most are aware. Bring the "feeling" of the experience into your awareness and let it open to you.

Sharing: This is a great start to the course for me. I feel like a childhood mystery has been solved. I am thankful for your answer, Kris. The early awareness I had has brought me confidence when things have been tough. I focused on the knowingness that I was part of a great mystery where the light resides. I am afraid that this connection sometimes made me reckless, since I have pushed the limits. Now I have become more receptive and adaptable to the original task. I will continue to hold attention on my declaration to Spirit. For the first time in many years, I can recall that optimistic and solemn situation.

Dreaming

Question: If life on this physical plane is a dream of our Dreamers, then what are those experiences during sleep that we also term dreams? Are they a form of 'reality' also dreamed by our Higher Self, but within a different band of existence?

Answer: To the dimension of physicality, dreams seem illusionary and temporary. In the same way, from the viewpoint of the Dreamer, our lifetime seems illusionary and temporary. However, just as when we are dreaming while asleep the dream seems real, living in a body seems real. One thing we find when we do this work is that often there are no words to describe properly what it is we are experiencing. This is one of those examples. The Dreamer dreaming our lifetime is not the same as when we dream when asleep, but this analogy does help us understand our life as a dream.

We are multidimensional beings. We have both Tonal and Nagual aspects, for example. We also have what Toltecs call our dream body, existing at a different dimension than our "awake" state. Part of our quest is to be able to place our awareness fully in any dimension of Self, whether we place it in our emotional body, in our Nagual aspects or in our dreaming dimension. The average person has most of their awareness locked in their mental body. They have some physical and emotional body awareness, and a tiny bit of dreaming awareness, with almost no awareness of their Nagual aspects.

While living in the earthlifesystem we access our point of power when we have our awareness centered in our physical bodies. From this point, we move our awareness out into other dimensional aspects of Self. For example, when you are having an outofbody experience or you are dreaming and you find yourself in an unpleasant situation, if you can find your physical body and move your awareness back to it, it is rare that anything in another dimension can harm you.

During dreaming, we actually enter another dimension that exists, but it seems that when we awaken it disappears. It does not. It is always there. I sometimes enter powerful vortexes of energy in my dreams. When I do, I intend to remember the sensation of that energy. As I go about my day, I just recall that energy sensation and I immediately pop right back into the dream, back into that energy vortex. It is as though by recalling the energy sensation I am able to walk through a doorway back into the dream. After a few days, the doorway begins to fade and usually closes.

Knowing That I Needed a Way Out

Sharing: When I was a teenager, it seemed that I was the only person who could not deal with the world...

After a series of different paths through school, and the ups and downs in life, I finally arrived at the Toltec Path. I signed up for the mailing list and saw this course. It just resonated on a mental level, and despite my misgivings about visiting my dark side again, I felt too drawn to the course not to take it. I have many patterns occurring now that I do need to break and replace with healthier thinking. I feel that a couple of years of hard work with a driving teacher could set me up for the rest of my life. Time will tell.

Answer: Continue to focus on those desires for healing, growth and evolution. When we follow these back far enough we find that they come from a part of Self that resides deep at our core. The desires are urges, higher aspects of Self urging you along your path. Following these urges will not lead you astray, and will guide you to where you need to be.

Question: Am I correct in thinking that these urges are aspects of the Higher Self/Dreamer pushing us towards what is best for us? That they appear as only urges and vague desires because we are not as in tune with our spiritual sides?

My urges are easy to find. It is staying on the path once I have found them that gets difficult!

Answer: Yes, as we move deeper into Self these urges become clearer. By holding them in our awareness, we open up the channel between higher aspects of Self/Dreamer and our surface awareness. When we follow the urges, the Higher Self/Dreamer is able to work through us, quickening our growth path.

Exercise II - Supplement to the Book of Life

Your first task is to begin to create your Book of Life, in which you are going to bring awareness, and explore original desires for growth.

However, why are you doing this?

The Toltec Warrior uses Intent for everything that they do. You are using Intent when you place your will behind your action. We can describe Intent as your purpose with your will behind it. Use Intent in everything you do, including beginning your Book of Life.

When you work on your Book of Life, think about your purpose for working on it, and allow this to drive you. Using Intent in this way adds to your power and creates stronger results.

Book of Life Sharing

Question: Regarding the Book of Life that we are starting, do you want to know the contents or is that for our own use only?

Answer: The Book of Life is for your own personal use. If you wish to share parts of it that is fine, but it is not required.

It sometimes helps to externalize our observations and realizations. When we put what we have observed or realized into writing, we clarify it and bring it into form. Once it is in form, we have the choice either to integrate it into our lives or to discard it.

Lesson II -   **The Authentic Self**

There is a part of us that knows. It is sometimes called the Authentic or Essential Self. At different times in our life, this part is more present, or closer to our surface awareness than at other times. When we clean, clear and heal ourselves, we reconnect with this part of Self.

Once we connect to it, we are able to monitor this Self first, and then live our lives. What most individuals do is monitor their outerworlds: the people, things, and situations. Most people monitor what is outside of them, and then try to change Self to fit in with the outerworld. This is backwards. Once we have awareness of the Authentic Self, we need to monitor the Self first, and then live our lives in accordance with the Self.

The reason for this is that our outerworld is the effect, not the cause. Our outerworld is, to a large degree, created by the Self and our innerworld. If our innerworld is in chaos, chances are our outerworld will soon be in chaos as well. The formula is to first monitor the Authentic Self, whose essence is truth and love, then align our innerworld to the Authentic Self. When we do this, our outerworld will follow our innerworld and reflect the Authenic Self in our lives.

When we monitor the outerworld and try to change Self accordingly, we are being controlled by the dream instead of creating the dream from a higher aspect of Self.

Lesson III -   **Love as an Essence**

When we move to the Nagual, we find that there exist essences. One such essence is love. An essence has no subject or object, and is unconditional. An essence is unstructured. When we bring an essence into the structure of the Tonal, it takes on conditions. This is the natural flow and process.

Dealing with essences is part of the Mastery of Intent, in which we work on bringing essences of the Nagual into the Tonal and our lives. This is beyond the scope of the Mastery of Awareness, but we will touch on it here.

One of the most beautiful aspects of this path is bringing essences of the Nagual into our lives. We do this through aligning the bodies of the Tonal to the essences of the Nagual. Love, abundance, freedom, power, peace, as well as essences that language does not have words for, exist in the Nagual. To bring them fully into manifestation in our lives we must first have a clean, clear, healed and strong human Tonal, and we must be able to perceive the Nagual. This preliminary work is what we are doing in the Mastery of Awareness and the Mastery of Transformation.

The problem with love, as we know it, is that it is twisted up in our emotional wounding. Most of what people call love is a form of codependence whereby the other person fills a hole in our Self where we have a wound. The problem with this is that it never heals the wound, and when the person goes away we are in pain.

In the Toltec Path, we are able to access pure love as an essence and incorporate it into our lives. Complete fulfilling love and freedom are two of the yummy things we can look forward to in this path.

Lesson IV - Beliefs, Knowingness, Knowledge

Silent Knowledge, or what I call direct knowingness, comes from the level of the Nagual. The mental body is part of the human Tonal. It vibrates too dense to perceive knowingness. Part of the process in the first two Masteries is freeing our awareness from the bodies of the Tonal the mental, emotional and physical bodies, so we are aware on the level of the Nagual.

We will speak more of this as we progress, but in brief terms, knowingness is unstructured. Knowledge is structured. The Nagual is unstructured. The Tonal is structured. The mental body is the first body of structure in the human Tonal. On a deep level, its purpose is to structure essences of the Nagual to bring them into form, or manifestation.

When we take unstructured knowingness and bring it into the mental body, it becomes structured knowledge. The mental body takes knowingness and gives it pictures and thoughts and it becomes knowledge. When Toltecs speak of Silent Knowledge, they are speaking of knowingness that is prethought, preconcepts and premental pictures. It is therefore silent. It resides on a frequency of energy above the mental body. You cannot think your way to the Nagual. You must free your awareness that is bound by your mental inventory, so you can perceive the Nagual at its level.

When you can access knowingness, you no longer need to go outside of yourself to books or people for answers, or go to your existing inventory for answers. It is a nice place to be.

Is Knowingness Like Intuition?

Question: Would this knowingness also be on the same lines as intuition or gut feeling? I know for me, sometimes a question/issue will come up and I will need guidance. If I can slow down, get the chatter in my head to quiet (which is still extremely difficult for me), I actually can physically feel changes in my lower abdomen, and sometimes I feel it in my chest. My chest feels very full.

There have been times that this "intuition" has been so strong that it almost seems like I can "see" what would happen if I were to go against it. And, the times I have listened to it and followed it, I have been so thankful.

Answer: Intuition and gut feeling are similar to knowingness, but employ different aspects of Self.

The intuitive body is one of the first bodies of nonstructure. There is a strong connection between our emotional body and our intuitive body. This is why women are sometimes more intuitive, because they have a tendency to be more centered in their emotional bodies than men do. This is a generalization, and everyone is different.

A gut feeling comes, as the name implies, from the gut or our body. In Japanese they have a word, "haragei", that is similar in meaning to gut feeling. Successful Japanese executives are said to develop haragei when making decisions. The decisions are not based on logic, but are based on a gut feeling. If we want to generalize, men are more prone to have a gut feeling as they generally are more physical bodyoriented, and women have more of a tendency to use their intuition. Again, this is a generalization, and both men and women can develop their gut feelings or intuitive body.

The physical body is able to sense things beyond time and space without thought. It is related to the instinctive center of the body. Animals use their instinctive center to know.

It is good to continue to develop your body sense. When you have a sense of things that you just know without thought, take note of the sensation in your body. The next time you wish to "know" something, try to recall the process and the same sensation.

Knowingness is somewhat different from intuition and gut feeling. You must rise in frequency to access knowingness. Knowingness is often large, like a huge ball.

It can take several days to for the mental body to unravel knowingness and bring it into structure.

Chapter II - The Nagual, The Tonal & PEM

Lesson I - The Nagual and The Tonal

It is 'candy for the reason' time again. Our reason loves to figure things out. We love to have answers. The truth is that real personal growth and spiritual evolution comes from the experience of the "doing" of the processes and techniques. Giving information and ideas does not add much to personal growth and, if we only take in more knowledge without applying it, it can actually do more harm than good. That being said, most of us love to hear and read knowledge. Therefore, to keep the mental body engaged we supply candy for the reason.

Briefly, the Nagual is all that is. Toltecs sometimes describe the Tonal as an island in the infinite sea of the Nagual. The Tonal is everything we know. In terms of energy, the Tonal is structured energy, or form. It is a condensation of the Nagual. All that is the Tonal comes from the Nagual. It is the Nagual manifest. The Nagual is unstructured. It has no form. It is both chaos and emptiness.

The focus of this course is our personal growth, evolution and empowerment. To this end we will focus on the human aspects of the Nagual and the Tonal – how they apply to us. Using this structure, we are able to increase our awareness of who and what we are. As human beings, we have both Tonal aspects and Nagual aspects. Our Nagual aspects are unlimited. Our Tonal aspects are our potential. When we are fully aware of both our Tonal aspects and our Nagual aspects, we have unlimited potential.

Spirit needs structure to manifest in physicality. The human Tonal provides that structure. However, for the Nagual to manifest through the human Tonal the Tonal must be clean, clear, healed and strong. The Toltec Masteries of Awareness and Transformation deal with the cleaning, clearing, healing and strengthening of our Tonal. We must, at least to a significant degree, complete this cleaning, clearing, healing and strengthening process before we embark on the Mastery of Intent. The Mastery of Intent deals with the Nagual aspects of Self, and aligning the Tonal to our Nagual aspects. We can call the Nagual aspects of Self our Divine Self. The Toltecs call it our Dreamer. We are the dreamed, dreamed by the Dreamer, and our life is the dream. We can also refer to the Tonal as our *human* side, and the Nagual as our *being* side. When complete we are a *human being.*

Can We Speak of the Nagual?

Question: When I read what you are writing I feel that I think more clearly. It is as though I wash my glasses to see what is in front of me and around me more clearly. If the Nagual is unstructured, does that mean that we cannot talk about it? I imagine that we could just live it with our body. Give me some explanation. I would like to know the link between expansion of consciousness, shamanic travel, visions and the Nagual.

Answer: The Nagual and shamanic travel, visions, expanded consciousness are all large topics in and of themselves. As we go along we will expand more on these, but I will try to touch upon them briefly.

First, we cannot *explain* the Nagual. It must be experienced at its level. It is beyond the comprehension of the mental body, which is the body that uses words and language. On the other hand, as we noted previously, we do need a structure when beginning our quest. Therefore, we attempt to provide a structure by *describing* what the Nagual is. However, we do not want to make the mistake of believing that we know what the Nagual is just because we have described a structure used to experience the Nagual...

Your notion that we can live the Nagual with our physical body is also correct. The physical body is not encumbered by our inventory (concepts, beliefs, words) that prevents us from perceiving the Nagual. Human beings are one of the only species that block themselves off from the Nagual. Toltecs call this phenomenon "selfreflection". We will be speaking more about selfreflection later. However, for now understand the Toltec term "selfreflection" has nothing to do with the traditional meaning of selfreflection, as used by other personal growth schools. In Toltec terms, selfreflection is the state where, when we try to perceive the Nagual, all we perceive is our inventory reflecting back to us. Animals do not suffer from selfreflection, as they are not trapped by their inventory as humans are.

Out of the bodies of the Tonal, the physical body is the one least encumbered by inventory or wounding, and for some people is the body that they can use to establish a link to the Nagual. This does depend on the person, however. Everyone is different. Most of us have our awareness trapped in the mental body, and do not have enough physical body awareness to establish the link.

Expanded consciousness consciousness is a mystery that is misunderstood. It is actually an aspect of the Nagual, and as such cannot be explained. When we speak of expanded consciousness, we are usually referring to expanded awareness. Awareness is something almost everyone is able to experience, and is the first thing we must free up and expand. It *is* the first step.

Shamanic travel shamanic travel, and dreaming, are tools we use to free up our assemblage point, which must become fluid to perceive and experience the Nagual. They can also help break the selfreflection of the mental body. The mental body is structured. Shamanic travel and dreaming are fluid, and can crack the selfreflection of the mental body.

Shamanic travel opens new worlds where we can find guidance and tools for life. Much more can be written about this. What is most important is that we apply the tools we receive in dreaming or shamanic travel to our daily lives, right here, right now. In addition, whether it is dreaming, outofbodies or shamanic travel, these are all enhanced and become much clearer when we have cleaned, cleared, healed and strengthened the human Tonal. Inventory and emotional wounding are dense, and can pervert our experiences in other worlds.

Work on the Tonal is not the fun part of the journey. However, if we are willing to take the time necessary to deal with this part of the work, the rewards are greater than we can imagine.

Lesson II - **PEM**

What is the human Tonal? The human Tonal consists of three bodies: the physcial body, the emotional body and the mental body [PEM]. Each body has its own particular function. The mental body's function is to think and picture. On a deeper level, its purpose is to structure essences of the Nagual. The emotional body's function is to feel. The physical body's function is to act and experience.

In the Mastery of Awareness, it is important to become increasingly aware of each body and its function. In western society, the mental body is held supreme, and we often use the mental body to suppress the other bodies. This is a form of dysfunction. Sometimes we attempt to use a particular body for a function that does not belong to it. For example, many try to "feel" with their mental body. This is not the function of the mental body. It is the function of the emotional body. Therefore, when a woman asks a man how he *feels* about something, he may answer by saying, "I don't know, let me *think* about it." This is cross functioning between the bodies of the mental and the emotional.

Our awareness must be able to move freely through our Tonal aspects. Many attempt to only place their awareness on their Nagual aspects. It does not work. First, until we clean, clear and heal our Tonal aspects, we are not able to perceive the Nagual clearly. We risk moving into fantasy. Second, we will not have enough personal power to manifest the Nagual fully in our lives. This is why some people of the new age generation have a tendency to be ineffectual in their lives. They can get into nice realms of energy, but their daily lives are shambles. Third, when we run high energy of the Nagual it shakes loose our unresolved emotional issues, charges and wounding. If we have not done the healing work necessary, the higher energy of the Nagual can overwhelm us by causing a loss of reference points and a collapse in our inner and outer worlds. This can be a painful and prolonged experience.

This is not said to invoke fear. When my nonphysical teachers ran high frequency energy through me, they called it turning up the energy. When they turned up the energy, my entire inner and outer worlds collapsed. I was in severe depression for more than two years. It was the most painful period in my life, but also the most magical. The turned up energy accelerated my healing process. It was as though I had a lifetime of healing work condensed into a couple of years.

As the light of awareness begins to move deeper into Self, it is common for repressed emotional wounding to come to the surface. Just know that this is part of the process. What we do not want to do is to attempt to suppress what comes up. It is better to process what comes up bit by bit than attempt to push it back down into our subconscious. If we continue to avoid, deny and suppress any part of Self, when we run high frequencies of the Nagual the suppressed parts can be pushed up all at once, causing much pain and overwhelming us.

The good news is that once you have cleared and healed your life, your dream begins to change dramatically. You move from the dream of the planet to the dream of heaven. You also clear the way for the Nagual to manifest in your life. Gifts, such as inner guidance, knowingness and "seeing", begin to show up more frequently. You are able to move your awareness freely into energetic realms, and the second attention. Work on our Tonal aspects is not always fun, but is well worth the effort.

Exercise I - Tuning into the Tonal

The following process is easiest to learn while guided, although you can do it on your own. [Information about CDs that contain the process is included at the end of the book.

Sit quietly and relax as if you were going into a meditation.

Become aware of your physical body. Feel its weight, any warm or cool spots, any places of tension just focus on your physical body and tune into it deeply. Become aware of your physical body as an entity in and of itself. Sense your gratitude for your physical body, the body that enables you to experience this life on Earth.

Now, tune into your physical body and ask it what it needs. Open and become receptive, and let it communicate with you. When you receive the answer, acknowledge it and let your physical body know that you will attend to its needs.

Shift your focus to your emotional body. Become aware of how you are feeling. What was your general mood during the day? What was your emotional tone during the last week? In general, what is your habitual emotional tone? Move deeply into your emotional body and feel your gratitude for it.

Now, tune deeply into your emotional body and ask it what it needs. Open and become receptive, and let it communicate with you. When you have the answers, acknowledge them and let your emotional body know that you will fulfill its needs.

Shift your focus to your mental body. What is it thinking? What state is it in? Is it active? Is it quiet? Notice how the sensation of your mental body is different from your emotional and physical bodies. Move deeply into your mental body and know your gratitude for how it has always helped you in life. Let it know that you are now connected to something larger in Self, and that you are in control. Let it know that it can relax now. Ask it to come with you in your quest.

Now, ask your mental body what it needs and let it speak to you. When you have the answers, acknowledge them and let your mental body know that you will fulfill its needs.

This process will strengthen your awareness in all areas of your life. It also brings health and wellbeing to the bodies of your Tonal. The more we exercise the muscle of awareness, the more it grows and expands. Try to do this exercise every day. You can also do a short version of this exercise by just taking a couple of minutes to tune into each of the bodies. You can do it while at work or at home. Doing this will keep you centered and less disconnected from Self.

Tuning into the Human Tonal

Question: I wanted to share an interesting observation about focusing on the bodies of the Tonal. Two weeks ago, I had signed up for a Tai Chi course that began that morning. I figured it would make a good connection to my physical body. The other two bodies must have been in turmoil over my attention being focused on physical and not mental or emotional, because my whole morning was foggyheaded and just felt weird. I was being judgmental for no reason, and found it hard to focus my mind on anything. Shortly into the class, I could feel the connection being made to my physical body, from that moment on my mind cleared, my thoughts slowed down, and I was focused in my physical body. Can the emotional and mental bodies get jealous of each other? Was this the emotional body showing itself to me? I am curious about this experience. Any ideas?

Answer: Tai Chi and other body awareness/movement exercises are good for balancing the system.

Sometimes when first bringing awareness to each body, we find, particularly with the emotional body, there are many accumulated charges. This sometimes can be uncomfortable, and it is part of the purpose of the exercise. As we bring awareness to each of the bodies, they begin to open and flow, making a clear channel for the Nagual to come through.

What is most important at this stage is just being aware of the state of each of your bodies, good or bad, pleasant or unpleasant. You are doing well.

Exercise II - Balancing the Bodies

When we tune into the bodies of the Tonal, we may find that they are out of balance with each other. Here is a simple exercise we can do at the end of the Tuning into the Bodies of the Tonal exercise.

Recall the sensation of each of the bodies, and visualize them sitting in front of you. You are sitting, and all three bodies are sitting next to each other facing you.

Notice each body. How do they look? Is one larger or smaller than the others are? Have a talk with them. Let them know that you need them on your journey, and you appreciate and love them. Ask them to come along with you on your quest. Ask them to work with each other in harmony. If one body is too large in comparison with the others, visualize it shrinking down. For any body that is small compared to the others, visualize it expanding.

When all the bodies are balanced, put your arms around them and pull them into Self.

This is a simple exercise, but it can be powerful. Note how each body feels the following day.

Tuning into the bodies of the Tonal

Sharing: I first tried to meet my three bodies: the physical, the emotional and then the mental. It was difficult. I felt as if they were people I had lived with for 37 years but had not spoken to before. Now I understand that this is the right thing to do with my different bodies, it is evident! Afterwards, I had them sit in front of me. It is a strange feeling to have "myself" in front of me.

When I live this way, this exercise changes my life. My mental body is very strong like an athlete, and it speaks a lot: it likes the word "him" a lot. My emotional body is like a shy woman, much too sensible and small. She is afraid to exist and to stand next to the mental. Therefore, I help "her" to take her place. I ask the mental to help her and to share "his" qualities with her. My physical body is like a nice animal; it is strong like a little bear, but a little primitive, savage. I ask the mental and the emotional bodies to share their qualities with it. Therefore, all the positive qualities of each body go to the others. I ask them to help each other and to work with Me to make the best "we" possible. Now we are a team! For example, today I had a problem with my physical body and I asked the three bodies what they thought, felt and acted so they could find a solution together.

For the first time, I have spoken with my physical body. It becomes less savage. However, I also like the savage strength. I asked them to keep their identities, to become less anxious and stronger. It is a good and powerful exercise.

Balancing the Bodies of the Tonal

Question: I just finished doing the CD exercise again as you suggested. What is happening for me in this exercise is that I keep noticing how exhausted my mental body is. Physically and emotionally, I am OK during the exercise, but when I get to the mental body, I feel so tired. This explains why I feel exhausted and cannot sleep when I go to bed at night; it is because my physical body is awake but my mental is the tired one. I am wondering if working on relaxing the mental body daily is a good focus, and if just this will strengthen the Tonal.

Answer: Thank you. This is a good observation. For many of us the mental body is continually overworked. Society emphasizes the mental body and discourages the other bodies, particularly the emotional body. Many of us were discouraged from expressing our feelings growing up, for example.

When the bodies of the Tonal are out of balance, it causes dysfunction and disease. Essences of the Nagual cannot flow through an unbalanced Tonal. One way to balance the bodies is to be aware of how we are unbalanced. Another is to be aware of how we crossfunction, as in the example of where we try to "feel" with our mental body. Another example is when we use the mental body to determine whether we "should" be hungry or not. To a large degree, many of us have lost touch with our physical body. We have suppressed its needs for many years and do not listen to it.

Another way to bring vitality to each of the bodies is to fulfill each body's needs. A simple example: if your physical body needs to urinate, listen to it and do not override it with your mental body. There are also energetic techniques we can do to balance the bodies.

Your realization of why you may have difficulty sleeping, even though you are mentally exhausted, is a good one. Your physical body's need of exercise may have been ignored, and it is not tired.

The bottom line is that we must begin to cease suppressing anything that enters our awareness, whether it is needs from the physical body or feelings from the emotional body. This does not mean that we indulge in our emotions. One reason why we may get into depressions or moods that are difficult to break is that we habitually use the mental body to suppress the emotional body. Our feelings become emotional charges that finally well up like a dam. When they finally do come out, they are out of balance and are difficult to deal with. If we fulfill the needs of the bodies of the Tonal in the moment, without suppressing them, we will bring our Tonal into balance.

Who/What is Tuning into the Bodies?

Question: This morning while doing the Tonal exercise, I had a delightful experience! I realized how much my body wants to be loved and respected, how much attention my mental body requires and demands, and how difficult it is to get in touch with my emotional body. Amidst all this, a beautiful sensation appeared. I felt I was expanding, growing larger, feeling free, and blending with the atmosphere. Then for some silly reason, I felt afraid and zapped back into regular awareness. Was this my dream body?

Answer: You, as well as some others who have shared their experiences, are beginning to experience who you truly are. We are not our physical, emotional or mental bodies. They are beautiful aspects of the human Tonal that enables us to experience physicality and manifest the Nagual in form. However, they are not who *we* are.

Do this exercise: after tuning into each of the bodies, become aware of *who/what* is tuning into the bodies. Move into the energy of the *who/what*. This, as with the connecting with our desires process, helps us connect to who and what we are.

Lesson III - **More on The Tonal and the Nagual**

The Nagual is all that is. The Tonal is merely a condensation of the Nagual. When we say, "go to the Nagual", or "bring the Nagual into the Tonal", it is simply a point of reference for the purposes of providing a structure for our growth path. The path of don Juan and the path we are describing here are the same path. The only difference is in the form, but even the form has little differences. The parasite will use the knowledge you have read in books to tell you something different. The parasite will attempt to block you from seeing the essence of the path.

This course deals with the first Mastery, the Mastery of Awareness. It is the first step, but a necessary one before we progress to the Masteries of Transformation and Intent. In the Mastery of Awareness, we begin with the Tonal. We must begin here to become aware of what binds us and keeps us from the Path of Freedom. In the Mastery of Intent, we "return" to the Nagual, and we bring the Nagual into our daily lives.

Don Juan's students also followed the same path. Moreover, he used a different approach for each. Ninety percent of Castaneda's books are about don Juan's attempts to break Castaneda's selfreflection – to shatter his preconceived ideas, knowledge and view of the world. This is work on the Tonal – the Masteries of Awareness and Transformation. Don Juan used drugs, and sorcerer's tricks to shatter Castaneda's shell, which was hard to crack. Taisha Abelar, Castaneda's cohort and also one of don Juan's students, was not given drugs. Instead, she had to do things like spending months in a cave recapitulating her Tonal.

The above sounds extreme, but it demonstrates just how important it is, even with don Juan, to do the work required on the level of the Tonal before we move into the Nagual.

Lesson IV - **Personal Task & Life Mission**

We all have a personal task and a life mission. Our personal task is selftoself. We come into this life with one or two core issues. Our family and society, primarily our parents, instill the wounding surrounding the personal task. By the time we are 6 or 7 years old it is set, and we spend the rest of our lives working it out.

This sounds a bit gloomy, but it is not really. In the beginning, it can be painful, but as we work them through, our wounds and weaknesses transform into our greatest strengths.

Our life mission is selftothe world. For a few, a life mission may be highly visible, such as a famous author or a rock star. For most of us, our life mission is not so dramatic, but, nonetheless, it is just as important.

The mistake often made is that we go for our life mission and avoid our personal task. Our personal task must, to at least some degree, be fulfilled before we embark on our life mission. If we skip over our personal task, our life mission becomes perverted and does not bring lasting fulfillment.

For example, perhaps our life mission is to be a famous musician to spread love through music. However, our personal task is to heal our selfworth issues caused by wounding due to a lack of love and acceptance by our parents. If we do not heal and fulfill our personal tasks, and try to jump to our life mission, our music may not carry the message of love, but instead may be highly negative. We may only be interested in the fame of being a rock star, and try to heal our wounding through the fame. It never works. We must begin with our personal task.

Castaneda had a life mission. Don Juan knew that a new era had come in which esoteric knowledge that had been hidden from society would now be available to all who sincerely desired it. He knew that Castaneda was to be the first messenger. Castaneda was a good messenger. He was a great storyteller, and presented Toltec knowledge in a way that hooked many people.

Exercise I - What is Your Personal Task?

In this course, we will be working with the power of awareness. Awareness comes from what Toltecs call our energy body, sometimes called the etheric body. Consciousness comes from the Dreamer. Consciousness follows awareness. This is a basic law. If we want to bring more consciousness into our lives, we engage our awareness.

Engage your awareness now and reflect upon your life. Notice patterns that have risen repeatedly in your life – areas that need healing. The Tonal (structured aspect of Self) is the foundation upon which higher aspects of Self rest. Many are always trying to go to Spirit (upward flow). While this flow is necessary, it is onehalf of the cycle. To complete the cycle we must be able to bring Spirit down into our lives (downward flow). Spirit needs structure to manifest into physicality. The human Tonal provides that structure. However, to *realize* the infinite, unstructured Nagual in our daily lives we must have a clear, clean, healed and strong Tonal. We must be clear channels for the infinite to manifest through, and we must be strong vehicles to maintain the infinite in our daily lives. Therefore, when we go up to Spirit, we must be certain we bring it back down through Self and into our lives.

Many people simply go up. They go up to higher aspects of Self and Spirit. And yes, it is a wonderful place to be. However, if they do not bring the infinite back down into their lives they split. They do great as long as they are up, but when they come back down to their daily lives they are in pain and suffering. If this pattern continues, soon running to Spirit becomes an escape from the structured aspects of Self. The Dreamer's dream becomes a waste. We waste a lifetime. Coming into body has an Intent, Purpose and Meaning. If we continually try to avoid the life experience, we never fulfill the Intent, Purpose and Meaning or our lives. The Toltec Path deals with both the unstructured, infinite Nagual aspects of Self; and the structured, Tonal aspects of Self. To become selfrealized we must realize our unlimited aspects of Self through our structured aspects of Self.

Engage your awareness as you go about the living of your life. Note recurring patterns, and anything in life that you have resisted, or that limits your freedom. Observe Self while holding the backdrop of personaltask. As you observe your life, what do you see that may relate to personaltask? What did you bring into this lifetime that needs healing and growth, selftoself?

Write down what you discover. It is important to externalize what you observe, and we externalize it through sharing it with others who have a common Intent of healing and growth, or by writing it out for ourselves. By externalizing what you observe, you clarify and bring it out fully into awareness.

Where I Need Healing

Sharing: Running to Spirit to escape the pain of daily life is something that I've done often, and still do. It is easy for me to get caught up in planning and focusing on my daydreams and what I think would make me happy. I often envision something, and get caught up in the feeling of it, but then I either abandon the idea, or I make only halfhearted attempts and then quit.

Also, your example talked of ending up split. This also I can relate to, having spent more time in my head than in my body. It is easy for me to stay caught up in the feeling of an idea, and not check back into my body and sort out whether or not it is something that I desire and is right for me to do.

The areas of my life that I believe need healing are relationships: with myself as well as with others; and belief in my own answers, that I know what is right for me. The growth area is reaching out and developing friendships (with both sexes) and relationships with women.

Response: One of the outcomes of this path is to find the place in Self where you can always go for answers. This is sometimes called the inner teacher. When you access your inner teacher (I sometimes call this my inner Nagual), the guidance is clear and always appropriate for the place you are.

One thing that is required is a trust in Self. Many of us lose our basic trust to one degree or another as we are domesticated. Also required is that we clean, clear, heal and strengthen the human personality aspect of Self, referred to as the Tonal. The Tonal is our foundation. The stronger our foundation, the higher we can go. But not only are we able to go higher, we are able to maintain the height, and we are able to bring it down fully manifest in our lives.

Working on Intimate Relationships

Sharing: When I think of what it is I came here to heal, the first thing that comes to mind is my intimate relationships with others, namely relationships with women. I find women difficult to approach because I don't know what to say; and if I do say something it always seems to be the wrong thing, and they give me a disappointed look. I end up feeling stupid, like I made a mistake and it further places me in a position of isolation. I've been alone for most of my life, but all of my deepest relationships with women that I loved and who I thought loved me turned out to be destructive.

Another thing is the type of women that I find to be intimate with. They are almost exactly the same type of personality, wanting to control everything; and even then will never be satisfied. It's always been a problem, and has spurred me on to find out what it is about me that is causing this to occur.

I've come such a long way in healing this, but still something doesn't "feel quite right" about it, and I know I need more healing in this area. Sometimes it feels as though I am searching for something else, and that this is a symptom of what is ailing me. And, a sense that I have lost myself somewhere along the way, and this is my way of finding that elusive self I know I used to be.

Response: Often in this timeframe, men who are on a spiritual path carry much feminine energy. This has nothing to do with sexual preference. It has to do with being receptive. Receptivity is necessary to receive Spirit or the Essential Self.

However, once receptivity and connection is obtained it becomes important to develop the masculine, assertive energy flow. Assertiveness is not the same as aggressiveness. The assertive flow is necessary to bring essences of the Nagual down into form, into one's life.

Hold in your awareness your energy in terms of feminine and masculine. If you have attracted women with a predominately masculine energy flow, be aware of this. Notice whether in life you take the lead, are assertive and outgoing; or stand back, receive, and let life and people come to you.

Chapter III - Stalking the Personality

Lesson I -   **Stalking**

When we speak about stalking, we are talking about a tool utilized by the Mastery of Awareness and Transformation. Stalking occurs when we observe our behavior in the same manner a jaguar stalks its prey. The jaguar will get to know the habits of its prey, the places where it sleeps, feeds and drinks water, when it is alone and when others accompany it. In doing this, the jaguar learns when the best and most effective time to hunt its prey is. The jaguar never allows the prey to know that he is there, as this would change the habits of the prey, causing the jaguar to lose its meal. Instead, he quietly observes his prey, until he knows its habits well enough to hunt it proficiently.

A Toltec warrior does a similar thing. We learn to stalk our own personalities. We observe our habits, our behavior and ourselves. We learn what our buttons are, what affects our behavior, and who affects our behavior. We need to observe ourselves without judgment. In the beginning, our goal is simply to observe, not change or influence what we are observing. For example, if we notice that we begin to act giddy and insecure when a certain individual is with us, and we judge this, then we will stop this behavior. In which case we will not be able to observe ourselves long enough to see why we behave this way, why this particular individual causes us to react this way and how this affects us. Just like a scientific experiment that requires the scientist not to interfere, we need to observe only, so we can observe the "raw data" of our experiments. This is the core of the Mastery of Awareness.Stalking Yourself Like a Jaguar

Begin to stalk Self as a Jaguar stalks its prey. At this point do not try to change what you see, just observe it. If you find something you do not like in yourself, do not judge it. Just note it, observe when and how it comes up. Stalking is bringing awareness to Self. Try to observe yourself at work, play, at home, when you relate to people, in all aspects of your life. Notice the patterns, behaviors, personality modes and so on. Notice your emotional state as you go about life. Notice any beliefs or patterns of thought. Notice your posture and body language. Witness your thoughts, feelings and actions in each moment.

Stalking Question

Question: So, as I understand the stalking exercise, we're simply observing. And, at this point, there's no action we need to take to report on, make note of, or adapt in any way... yes?

Answer: Yes, at this point we are a "witness", an impartial observer. We do not want to try to change what we see, as it is too easy to fall into the Judge/Victim syndrome, which we will be speaking about later in the course.

If you wish to note patterns that you see, you can do so in your Mitote Book, which will be introduced with the Judge/Victim, but be careful not to place any judgment on what you observe.

Exercise II - Be Aware That You Exist

When you wake up in the morning, be aware of Self. Just be aware that you exist in the body that is breathing, waking up. You, Self, exist as you get up to go to the bathroom, and get ready for your day.

Continue to remember that you exist as long and as often as you can during the day. Keep your awareness engaged on you, the Self, existing.

Love is Deeper Than a Feeling

Question: My problem is I don't get emotional over things. I've felt anger twice, a long time ago, but depression, melancholy, anxiety, sadness...things like that I have never felt. I'm usually happy, and take most things in stride, so I have no clue about this emotional body. Perhaps I've just never used it? I can feel love, I know that one real well, but the others escape me. And, I haven't had by any stretch of the word a bad childhood. Perhaps if I just focus on the feeling of love, that will suffice.

Answer: You make a good observation that you do not "feel" most emotions, but you do feel love. Later in the class, we will discuss feelings vs. emotions vs. essences, but for now let us say this:

Essences are different from feelings, and love is an essence, not a feeling. That is why you feel love but not other feelings.

Later we will go through an exercise to become more in touch with your feelings and emotions. However, it is important to remember that we can only access higher aspects of Self, or our Nagual, when we have cleaned, cleared and healed. Women and men of power have strong emotional bodies because they have included all of Self (their physical, emotional and mental aspects). We need to be in touch with all three bodies, and this means being aware of our feelings and emotions. This does not mean we allow our feelings and emotions to lead our lives or behavior, but rather it means being "complete" so our Nagual can come through us. As you said, men tend to be more thinkers than feelers. Do not judge this either way: we all have strengths and weaknesses, and the name of this game (life) is to work on healing, clearing and cleansing ourselves.

Lesson II - Emotions versus Feelings

There is a difference between emotions and feelings. This is a little more advanced stalking work, but if you can it is good to note the difference when stalking.

Feelings are natural. They arise naturally from the emotional body. Feelings are things like happiness, sadness, anger, joy and so on.

Emotions are charges. They are similar to feelings, but are charged by memories and woundings. If someone pushes your buttons, and they frustrate you, you are in an emotional charge, for example.

Feelings flow easily through us. Once expressed, they dissipate. Emotions have a charge to them and become stuck in us. Anger can be an emotion or a feeling. If you are habitually angry, it is a charge due to a wound, and is an emotion. If someone cuts in front of you in line, you may get angry. If you express it and let it go, the anger is a feeling. If you hold on to it, and think of all the other times you have had an injustice committed against you, you are in an emotional charge.

When stalking our beliefs, we may find that more times than not, a belief will have an emotional charge behind it. Moreover, the emotional charge will have a wound behind it.

We do not want to spend our time analyzing this too much. Just stalk the emotional body. If we always try to figure out what we are observing, we have lost the stalking stance. Just observe. The more you observe, the more understanding comes.

By the time they are adults, due to their wounding most people have lost the ability to feel. Their feelings are buried by emotional charges. This is a large impediment on a spiritual path, because our emotional body connects us to the heart chakra and the body of intuition. For many, part of the beginning work is to rehabilitate their ability to feel.

A common mistake people make on the spiritual path is to avoid their emotions, and in the process avoid their feelings. Some meditation processes actually encourage not feeling. This is detrimental to the path, as they cut off an essential part of Self – the feeling body. The reason for this is that they confuse emotions and feelings. Emotional charges will take you offcenter. Feelings are actually part of being oncenter.

When stalking our beliefs, we may find that more times than not, a belief will have an emotional charge behind it. In addition, the emotional charge will have a wound behind it.

We do not want to spend our time analyzing this too much. Just stalk the emotional body. If we always try to figure out what we are observing, we have lost the stalking stance. Just observe. The more you observe, the more understanding comes.

We lose energy through emotional charges energy we need for our growth. It takes much energy to grow and evolve. Feelings on the other hand help energy move freely through us.

Emotions belong to the falsepersonality. While they are normal, they are not natural. Feelings, on the other hand, are natural to the Authentic Self.

As you stalk yourself, be aware of the feelings and emotions that come up. Note the differences. See if you can distinguish between the two.

Moving Thru Self to Connect with the Nagual

Sharing: Awhile back, I came to understand how superficial the physical (Tonal) is compared to the overall (Nagual). This led me to tend to "disregard" as trivial the physical effects, thinking that they were for the most part illusory. I began to have problems with others who were hung up on their emotional difficulties, as these would frustrate me. I would try, (to no avail) to reason with them, demonstrating that the emotional pain they carried quite possibly contributed to their pain rather than working to alleviate it. Well, of course, this would aggravate their emotional condition and add to my frustration.

Getting to the point... Indirectly, while practicing this process (while driving in the car), I saw how deeply rooted the emotional body is. It is NO triviality. While I was becoming frustrated over a "slow driver", I caught myself. I asked, "why am I getting so frustrated?" I didn't have anywhere to go, where five minutes mattered. I realized the other had no sense of frustration/difficulty. He was a different person with different ways of looking at things. That is when it dawned on me! Down to the minutest detail, it's the emotional body that makes the biggest difference in the perception of each individual. If there's just the right combination of smells and colors in the environment, for example, I myself will see things differently than if, for instance, it's rainy, dark and dreary outside. But, the reality of all things, of the Nagual, is independent of these influences. Yet we, each and every one, paint it with "our" colors.

The physical is not at all trivial in the scheme of things for the human being. But yes, it is illusory. Seeing through to the truth gave me all the more incentive to forge ahead, to clean and clear more, to get an even better picture of this marvelous truth.

Answer: Yes, the emotional body is where most of us get snagged. Moreover, most of us have suppressed the body since childhood. We live in a dense timeframe. This timeframe is considerably less dense than, say, the Middle Ages several hundred years ago. However, it is still dense compared to how humanity will be several thousand years from now. Density is characterized by dysfunction in society, and due to the density of this timeframe, growing up we are all wounded emotionally. From the time we are young we begin to repress our emotional pain, pushing it deep into our subconscious.

When something is in our subconscious, we simply are not *aware* of its existence. However, just because we are not aware of its existence does not mean it does not influence our lives. Our emotional wounding, which we are largely unaware of until we progress with this work, actually controls much of our lives.

The emotional body is denser and more powerful than the mental body. It is much easier to change your mind than try to change a depression or a mood. From a deep level, beyond our awareness, our emotional wounding controls us. This manifests in the form of emotional charges, such as buttons that others can push. Many of our convictions and beliefs, even though they exist in the mental body, when followed back have their roots in our emotional wounding. Most are unaware of this connection and support their beliefs, convictions and opinions with mental justifications and reasoning, but what is going on is that an emotional wounding is controlling the belief or conviction.

Part of the Mastery of Awareness involves moving our awareness deeper into the subconscious. As we do, our "stuff" comes to the surface to be processed. This is a natural process of expanding our awareness. Moreover, it is a necessary one if we are to reconnect with our core being. Our core being lies at the depth of Self. It is covered and blocked off from our awareness by our wall of emotional wounding. We must go through this wall to reconnect with Self. Ultimately, to relink with the Nagual we must connect *through* our Essential Self.

Emotions vs. Feelings

Sharing: The following was a problem that I encountered recently, in regard to feeling anger.

It all started with our baby, then three months old, who was going to stay in the hospital for one night to be tested for risk of crib death. While I did not feel good about it from the beginning, I relaxed because my partner stayed in a separate room in the hospital. The nurse was treating our little baby in a very impersonal way. Seeing this I got angry. This was a feeling. I became firm with the nurse, almost rude, trying to get her to wake up just a little more.

The day seemed to have gone well; our daughter was not at risk for crib death. Two days later, it struck me that something was wrong with her: she was way too weak, too short of breath, and her crying was usually much more energetic. I took her temperature, which was too high for her age. The next morning her temperature was still too high, so we took her back to the hospital...

As I sat and considered her symptoms, it hit me: I knew that it had to be a virus she probably caught in the hospital two days prior. Although I was right, the doctor was unaware that it was a virus and ran Xrays, which were *unnecessary. When I found out about the Xrays, I was simply furious! Whitehot anger rushed through my body.*

That anger must have been an emotion. I can forgive people, but I always have a hard time when confronted with "systems", because there is not much you can do, or act upon.

Answer: We should all read the post of your experience several times. Anger can be a feeling. It is a natural response. You needed anger to "wake up" the nurse. You expressed it, and it passed through you and created the response you needed in the nurse.

Anger can also be an emotion. Many of us have an emotional charge that has built up about the feeling of powerlessness when confronting "the system". We react with anger and it does not release. Sometimes our reaction is inappropriate for the situation. From a personal growth aspect, we lose much energy needed for our growth.

Feelings are a response. Emotions are a reaction. We respond naturally with feelings, but when we have an emotional charge we react. When we are reacting to something, we lose sight of what it is. All we see is our reaction. So, if someone accidentally pushes one of our emotional buttons, we react. It may be that the other person's intent was positive. But due to our pentup emotional charge we react and are blinded by our reaction to the other's true intent.

The feeling anger can be transformed to motivation. If you find yourself angry, look at where you can use the anger to motivate yourself to take action.

How to Become Aware of Feelings and the Emotional Body

Question: I am having a little difficulty with this one. I can clearly focus on my physical body and I can clearly focus on my mental body, but the boundaries of my emotional body are not clear. For some reason I don't feel or exhibit much in the way of emotion. Other people have told me about this too. Can you offer any advice about this?

Answer: Many people, particularly men but also many women, have been taught to shut down their emotional bodies. By the time they are adults they have pretty much succeeded in doing so. Often we "think" we feel, but we are trying to feel with our mental body without knowing it.

When we focus our awareness on our emotional body, as distinct from our mental or physical bodies, it seems like there is nothing there, or we cannot really perceive it from the rest.

Try this. When doing the process, recall a very emotional experience, perhaps something that was sad in your life. Perhaps a loss you had. *Feel* that sadness. When you have the *feeling*, let go of the memory of the events and people around that feeling, and just focus on the feeling.

Try to hold on to this feeling for a period of time. Now go back to your mental body and become aware of it, the thinking body. Now switch back to the feeling and notice the difference between the two. Try to notice the difference in the energy sensation between the thinking body and the feeling body.

As you go about your day, try to *feel* things. Try to feel how a piece of news you hear affects you. Find a person or thing you love. Tune into how you *feel* about this person or thing.

As you do this, you will "reawaken" your emotional body. As we spoke about earlier, the emotional body is an essential part of intuition. With your emotional body activated, you will perceive much more of the world around you.

Exercise I - Find Your True Self

What most people identify with is not the Tonal, it is the false personality. The false personality comes from our domestication. It contains our subconscious wounds and all of the pain we have suppressed.

While we are inbody, the Dreamer and Nagual aspects of Self come through the Tonal to bring the unknown aspects of life into the known. The Tonal is the vehicle. Nagual aspects of Self cannot experience life, except through the vehicle.

It is as if we went to a foreign country, and their only means of transportation was a horse and carriage. The country is large, and if we wish to travel across it we must use their means of transportation the horse and carriage.

The Tonal is the horse and carriage in the earthlifesystem. To bring the Dreamer down into this world it must go through the Tonal.

We are challenged by this. First, we believe the false personality is the Tonal. It is not. It is false. Integrating the false personality is part of the cleaning, clearing and healing of the Tonal.

Second, and this is common among those on a spiritual path, due to the pain of the false personality we avoid the Tonal and constantly try to run back to Spirit.

This defeats the purpose of coming into body in the first place. We simply will not make movement on our path because we never use our vehicle, the Tonal.

Get in touch with your Tonal, your physical, emotional and mental bodies. Can you communicate with each? Are you able to observe them? When do you run to Spirit? What do you do to avoid the pain of the false personality?

Going In

Question: I just received the CDs, and last night was able to do the exercise at the end of the second CD. It was a painful experience, and the need to cry was uncontrollable when acknowledging the needs of the emotional and mental bodies. I was unable to decipher exactly what those needs were, but obviously they are strong. I shall be repeating this exercise everyday, however much it hurts.

I do have two questions: Kris, you said there is usually one particular state of mind or state of being where we individually tend to level out, which can be either joy, sadness, depression (which is my particular case), etc. Does this individual state of consciousness have any special reason/meaning, depending on whether we feel joy, sadness, depression?

Also, whenever I am about to begin some BIG questioning in my life, which can be regarding myself and personal problems or the reason for the existence of mankind.... it doesn't matter... I go into periods of needing to be alone. I get snappy with my husband and little boy; I need to be very quiet, with myself. I do not need food during these periods, which can last anything from a day to a week. I tend to shut myself in my room and stay there... contemplating, sleeping, dreaming, feeling, crying, and finally comprehending whatever it was that I needed to receive an answer for. My husband and son are now used to these periods, but I would still like to understand why they occur... Can anyone shed any light on this for me? Has anyone else experienced anything like this?

Answer: Our habitual emotional tone is just where we are. As we clean, clear and heal, it is natural for this emotional platform to begin to rise. We begin the cleaning, clearing and healing by bringing our awareness to the different aspects of Self, as we are doing in these processes. As our emotional platform begins to rise, a byproduct is personal power and the ability to have impact on your world.

As we have mentioned, we live in a dense timeframe. We are all wounded due to the dysfunctional society we are raised in. There is no judgment here. It isn't good or bad. It is just what is. There is a positive side to this. As we do the work to heal ourselves, we grow. This growth makes us stronger in ways we could never achieve without going through the healing process. Our weaknesses become our greatest strengths.

As for your wanting to be alone when confronting big issues, it is your process of going into the depth of Self. It is difficult for us to go deep within, because of our wounding. From the time we are young we bury our painful experiences deep inside and seal them away. When we go into our innerworld, we must, to some degree, penetrate the inner wall we have built to hide our pain.

As we do our healing, it becomes easier to bring awareness deeper into the depths of Self, and access our "true" Self which lies at our core.

The healing process isn't easy, and it isn't the fun part of this path, but the rewards are beyond our imagination.

Stalking position

Question: I just wondered at what position you would place the stalking awareness (of Self in this case). From this position, is it possible to stalk the mental processes and silence them; go to the emotional body and feel; and go to the physical body and sense? Would you place that stalking awareness in the mental, in the emotional, or in the physical body? I mean, you don't have to think to stop the thinking, for instance, which would tell us that it is not in the mental body. On the other hand, when I stalk my own mental processes I end up picturing things when, for instance, I am "listening" to my body. This, then, would speak in favor of the fact that the position of the stalking awareness is closer to the mental body when stalking the mental body, closer to the emotional body when stalking the emotional body, and closer to the physical body when stalking the physical body. However, I find the stalking position is somehow already closer to the "Nagual", and somehow away (or above) from the three bodies. I would like to have your opinion on this: is it your experience that the more fully one can engage all three bodies, the more the stalking position naturally moves closer towards the "Nagual"?

Answer: You are correct: ideally, the "stalking position" is closer to the Nagual. Awareness is an interesting thing. The more we "stalk" awareness, the more we find that it has many aspects. For example, we can split awareness we can focus our awareness on our mental body, while at the same time being aware of the Self. This is called selfremembering or selfpresence, Exercise II in this chapter.

When stalking the bodies of the Tonal, we can move into the bodies and become them, such as 'I think', 'I feel', etc., or we can witness them, as in 'it (the mental body) thinks', 'it (the emotional body) feels'.

One of the stances most conducive to personal growth and evolution is to hold a piece of our awareness continually on the Self that awareness originates from, while at the same time objectively observing (stalking) our thoughts, feelings, actions, attitudes, etc. This is slightly more advanced work than where we are presently at in this course, but some will be able to relate to it.

Getting to Know You

Sharing: It's difficult for me to speak with my physical body. In the beginning, I thought of it as an instrument; something used to walk, to move, to eat, to run. I feel shy speaking with him because I don't know "him" as a person, an entity. My mental always says that my body is important; I must take care of it. I realize that it is an entity. This realization is new and very nice. I am always with it; it feels like a friend, a twin. For now, I'm only able to speak with my physical body. I can feel my emotional body, but not as an entity. I can think my mental body, but not as an entity in and of itself.

Response: It is wonderful to take the time to get to know each of your bodies. Our physical body is a faithful friend that enables us to experience the world we live in. Spending time with our physical body, fulfilling its needs, and letting it know the love and gratitude we have for it, enhances our experience of the world and gives health and vitality.

Lesson III - Completing Cycles

Completing cycles is vitally important on our path. From early on, Toltecs understood the importance of hunting power and reclaiming our energy. It takes an incredible amount of energy to make movement on a spiritual path. Many people are stuck, simply because they do not have enough energy to proceed. They lose energy in many areas. There are energetic processes we can do to reclaim our energy and draw it back to Self, but one fundamental area of energy loss is incomplete cycles.

My nonphysical teachers would often say, "If you are looking for perfection, you have come to the wrong planet. The earthlifesystem is a system of completion, not perfection."

There is a bigger purpose for our being in body during this timeframe. This purpose has to do with the Dreamer completing what it needs to move to its next level. On an individual level, this means that by focusing our intent on completing whatever it is we need to complete, we will speed up our growth and evolution.

Exercise I - What Cycles do You Need to Complete?

Look at your life and see where you have openended cycles. Do you have clutter in your house or office that you have been meaning to organize? This is an incomplete cycle. Do you have projects that you have started but never finished? Do you have books you have started to read but never completed?

Life consists of cycles. A cycle is a beginning (birth), a duration (life) and a completion (death). Sunrise to sunset is a cycle. The new moon to full moon is a cycle. Our body consists of cycles. One resistance we have in completing cycles is our fear of death, of something ending. However, unless we complete the cycle we are in we are unable to move on to something better.

For example, some want a new relationship. However, they are still hanging on to an old relationship that they know isn't serving them, or has no future. What they don't realize is that until they bring the old relationship to completion, a new relationship cannot be born.

We have incompletion everywhere in our lives. We have energy stuck. The more incomplete cycles we have, the more we are draining our precious energy. We become stuck and powerless.

Start with small things. Find small cycles in your life that you can complete. It can be as simple as folding the laundry you have been putting off. Or it can be going through old bills and correspondence. Be aware of where you have open cycles, and bring them to completion.

By doing this you will not only free up your energy, but will find new probabilities opening up to you.

Who's Thoughts?

Question: I stalked myself all week during the meeting, and love this exercise! My realization is that I'm bored with my job and ready to move on. Now to complete the cycle! Wow, what a powerful thought.

I have found that when I hear talk from people, I know they are just thoughts...their thoughts. I have followed thoughts in the past and found them not to be true. I'm cynical these days, and take many statements with a grain of salt. I even question my own thoughts. Where does this come from? How do you tell the difference between parasitic thought and true thought? Does truth exist forever?

Answer: Good stalking. Most of the mental chatter we have in our heads is a result of our domestication. The best thing to do is to continue to stalk thoughts, and you will begin to be able to discriminate between which thoughts are simple reactions to things based on our conditioning, or something that comes from a deeper level.

For most people, thoughts are automatic. There is no intention in the thought. They are not "thinking." True thinking requires intention and awareness. When we are lost in our thoughts, we are lost. The Authentic Self does not exist in that moment. Without the Authentic Self, there can be no truth.

Life is Cyclical

Question: I have noticed that there are patterns in my life that keep coming up, and perhaps they become more challenging too. Can you comment on this?

Answer: It is great that you have the awareness that your life is cyclical, because often people run into the same problem over and over in life, and can't figure out why the world is such and such a way.

What is happening is that life is trying to help us see ourselves by mirroring our problems to us. And you see that life seems to go smoothly and then roughen up over and over. Yes, there are many layers to our growth. As we grow, we evolve and spiral up. We are all generally born with one or two life issues, which manifest in various different ways. Basically, we do have the same issues our whole lives, but we (hopefully) grow and evolve, so the problem does too. As children we had few problems, to the eyes of an adult, but children also have less developed "tools" to deal with their problems. A five year old child cannot think, because the mental capabilities are still being developed.

So, yes, as we grow and evolve our plate feels fuller. However, our ability to work with it increases too. Spirit never gives us more than we can handle, although it may feel otherwise.

As far as the positive side of things goes, our problems feel bigger than the good things in life. If you looked at your life and focused on the good, you would find that it too grows proportionally with you.

Chapter IV - The Parasite

Lesson I -   The Judge and the Victim

There is a mechanism within us that, from the time we are children, begins to take on a life of its own. Toltecs call this the parasite. The parasite robs us of energy needed for our personal growth and evolution. It vibrates dense, holding us down in the suffering of the dream of the planet.

One of the footholds of the parasite is what the Toltecs call the Judge and the Victim. When we bring awareness to the Judge and the Victim, we begin to realize just how pervasive it is in the internal dialog of our mind. The Judge is the voice in our heads that continually tells us what we should and should not do. It tells us we are not good enough. It chastises us when we make a mistake. It beats us up when we fail.

The Victim is the polarity of the Judge. When we fail at something, the Victim feels bad and worthless. When we feel guilty because we have not done something we "should" have done, we are the Victim. The Judge and the Victim are continually at work. The parasite even works its way into our personal growth. How many times have you felt you were not as far as you should be on your personal growth path? Have you every beat yourself up for not meditating enough or falling into the same pattern again? This is the parasite. It lives off the negative emotions created by the Judge and the Victim.

We begin to rid ourselves of the parasite by first stalking it. We observe the voices in our head that tell us what we should and should not do. We simply witness our patterns of beating ourselves up when we feel we have made a mistake, when we have failed, or when we have not been "good" enough.

When stalking the parasite we must be careful not to fall into its most common trap. When we stalk ourselves we become aware of our weaknesses, our negative emotions and patterns. We become aware of how we lose energy and how habitual our patterns are. When we become aware of this, it is easy for us to feel bad about ourselves or fall into selfpity. We may begin to beat ourselves up for all of the things we become aware of. This is the trap. As soon as we start to beat ourselves up, or feel bad about ourselves, we have just fallen into the Judge and the Victim, and we are being controlled by the parasite.

This is why it is critical to maintain the stalker's stance – to observe as an impartial witness. By maintaining the stalker's stance, we bring awareness to Self without falling prey to the parasite.

Exercise I - The Mitote Book

The word Mitote is akin to an open marketplace. An open marketplace is full of voices and noise. A Mitote is the chaos and noise of our minds. For the human, the Mitote is the realm of the parasite.

In the Mitote Book, we log our observations of the parasite. We do this to externalize it. When we externalize it, we move out of chaos and confusion and into structure. Putting it into words and onto paper gives it external structure, and moves it out of confusion and into clarity. The parasite thrives on confusion. Externalizing it by writing it down pierces the confusion.

As you stalk the Judge and the Victim, write what you see in your Mitote Book. Observe the voices in your head that say, "You should have ____; You shouldn't have ____; You should have done better; You didn't do well enough; You always make mistakes; You are too slow; You are behind in your growth; You are not smart enough," and so on.

Make two columns in your Mitote Book. Label the left column "The Judge." Label the right column "The Victim." Anytime you notice the Judge in yourself, write it down in the left column. Then note how you feel when the Judge speaks, and write down how the Judge makes you feel in the Victim column.

Stalk the Judge and the Victim. If you find a thought such as "I'm not good enough; I'll never make it; I'll fail." or "They won't like me," and so on, note it in your Victim column.

The Mitote Book is a great tool to bring the negative patterns we carry in our innerworld out into our outerworld, so we can release them.

Compassion

Question: When I first heard the notion of the parasite, Judge, and Victim, I was intrigued. I always thought that this was who I am. But I can see how these mechanisms serve the ego. This is how my ego has built, as don Juan says, its bubble of perception. A bubble, when not allowed to expand, only proves to limit.

As I have progressed along my growth path over the years, I was never aware of the parasite, Judge and Victim. Thus, I was really trying to progress by looking forward to building a "beautiful ego." A beautiful ego that was in fact dreamed up and designed by the ego itself. What a trap! It is so important to realize that this is not our Essential Self. The ego is mere fantasy, but at the same time it creates a fantasy that is experienced as being utterly real.

About a month and a half ago, I faced a challenge that had been weighing me down for seven years. I conquered it, and enjoyed the victory for about two minutes before it started a chain reaction that recently resulted in my girlfriend of 3 years, someone I had believed would be my wife, splitting up with me because I had kept this (and a few other things) from her. "I" have been experiencing much pain because of our breakup, even though I can see how much courage it took to liberate myself from the lies I had been living. The whole experience is forcing me to find compassion for myself. Is compassion the antidote for the Victim? Alternatively, is compassion the parasite telling us that everything is going to be okay? Furthermore, can compassion be viewed as an emotion/feeling that is an antidote to the Victim as long as there is no internal dialogue attached? Or, is my desire to reason this out getting the best of me...?

Answer: There comes a point in our lives when we must rid ourselves of our lies. It is never a fun process, and it shakes up our innerworld, which, in turn, affects our outerworld. Clearing our lies creates a clear channel for higher aspects of Self to come through.

Compassion in its pure form is an essence of the Nagual. It is healing in nature. To experience compassion we must, to at least some degree, break free from the parasite. The parasite turns compassion into feeling sorry for ourselves, and selfpity.

One way to access compassion is to recall a child, or a person that you feel compassion for. It does not need to be someone you know. Perhaps it is the plight of a hungry child you saw on television. Find the energy of that compassion and apply it to yourself. When done properly, compassion flows from the Essential Self to heal and nurture the wounded Self.

More Compassion

Question: La Gorda's words baffled me (Carlos Castaneda's "The Second Ring of Power", page 311): "The Nagual had taught us all to be warriors. He said that a warrior had no compassion for anyone. For him, to have compassion meant that you wished the other person to be like you, to be in your shoes..." They come to me when I read what you wrote. What to think of them?

Answer: Every lineage has a slightly different approach. The lineage of don Juan does not speak much of love, and does not use compassion in the same way that the lineage of don Miguel Ruiz uses love and compassion, for example.

Love and compassion are essences of the Nagual. Because we live in a dense timeframe, it is difficult to realize essences. There is just too much dysfunction in the dream of the planet. What most people believe is love is no more than filling the holes in each other's wounds; codependency. The same applies to compassion. When the average man or woman feels compassion for another, what is really happening is that the pain they perceive in the other stimulates the wounds they have in themselves. It is not true compassion.

In order to realize true love and compassion, we must have done the work to clear, clean, and most importantly, heal our wounded Tonal. We begin with the Mastery of Awareness, where we become aware of our wounds, patterns and stuck place: then we move to the Mastery of Transformation, where we heal and dismantle the false, wounded Self.

In the Mastery of Intent, when we have a clear, strong Tonal to act as a channel for Spirit or the Nagual to come through, we begin aligning Self to essences of the Nagual. It is at this point that we are able to realize essences such as love, compassion, freedom, all knowing, and so on.

The Nagual don Miguel Ruiz calls the Mastery of Intent the Mastery of Love, because in this Mastery we are working with essences such as love that are innate to the Nagual.

True compassion from Don Juan?

Sharing: I've been following this thing about compassion for a while now. My first impression still stands in my experience. I sense true compassion to be a sort of ray of "lovelight" coming from the source (true love) and piercing into "darkness" (the madness of the dream of the world).

Don Juan's eyes pierced ruthlessly into the darkness of Carlos, but if it was true compassion then did he make the mistake of helping out a seemingly lost Carlos?

I also believe that it is a bit premature to try to explain things like true love and true compassion to people that are still firmly entrenched within the separate Self/ego mind. With premature I mean that it will not help them out one bit along the path, except when one can honestly recall past glimpses of true love/compassion. To me that explains why it was not a part of the teachings of don Juan.

Answer: Yes, love and compassion are byproducts of a path of the heart. They cannot be explained, and can only be described to a limited degree. When I read don Juan working with Carlos, I sense much compassion coming from don Juan.

No Need to Go Digging

Question: I have dedicated some time to try to hear the parasite, the Judge. Instead of beginning to see patterns or hearing judgments, I am having great meditations, and I feel peaceful and blissful.

I need some help trying to stalk myself.

Answer: You do not need to go digging for the parasite. All you need to do is keep your awareness engaged, so when it comes up you will be aware of it.

If you are having sensations of peace and connection, then by all means align to them. Do not let the parasite tell you that you do not deserve them.

As long as we are not in avoidance or denial, we do not need to go digging for our patterns. They will come up of their own accord as we continue to shine our light of Awareness deeper into Self.

Congratulations

Sharing: I had not experienced the parasite this strong before I am loosing my pace. I am feeling overwhelmed by the amount of information, and have frozen since last week. I am shocked, feeling the claws of the parasite paralyzing my being. My day to day is becoming chaotic, my stalking is loosing strength I feel I am loosing energy in all levels. It feels terrible. Also, I perceive someone having a good time during my misery: the parasite is happy; because I am afraid I will not keep up with the group and the teachings. I just realized the parasite was sleeping for a long time, and I do not know how to deal with it.

Answer: Although you may not feel like it, you are at a good place. When we begin to break the parasite we break many of the reference points that we have based our reality on.

It feels like we are going crazy. It is overwhelming, and can be fearful. Just know the old Self is dying so the new Self can emerge. The new Self has a different set of rules it plays by. We cannot rely on our old patterns. When we begin to break the parasite, it kicks and screams. It causes chaos in our inner and outer worlds.

Just know there is light at the end of the tunnel. Trust the process and just be with the process. Connect with your desires for growth. Light a candle, sit with your altar if you have one, and connect with the group. Know that you have much help from many different sources.

Exercise II - The Mitote Book Supplemental

The ego is the false personality we have built up over a lifetime. It is the body of pretension. It pretends to be something it is not. The Judge/Victim/critical parent is just one aspect of the ego/parasite.

The parasite tends to mimic the personalities of the people around us as we grow up. We take on aspects of their personalities. Perhaps you have a parent that tries to put on a good face in difficult situations, instead of looking at the situation as it really is. Your parasite may adopt this attitude, "there is nothing wrong here, I'm fine, and the situation is fine."

This type of personality can maintain this upbeat attitude for a while, but has a tendency to swing down into despondency and depression.

At this point just keep your awareness engaged. Observe yourself and your reactions to people and situations during the day. If you find a pattern, just note it in your Mitote Book. However, do not try to overanalyze it. The parasite loves to analyze things. It tells you that if you analyze it you will heal it. Actually analyzing has nothing to do with healing.

You do not necessarily need to stick to the 2 column Judge/Victim in the Mitote Book. If you see a pattern in yourself, note it. If you do see a Judge/Victim pattern, note that in the 2 columns.

Observe things like:

Buttons that you have that others can push.

Judgments about others; no matter what they are.

Negative selftalk, inner dialog.

Be aware of your different moods during the day/week.

As you shine the light of Awareness on the parasite, it will begin to shake loose and come out of hiding. It sometimes starts slow.

Moreover, watch when the parasite says, "This is stupid, and it doesn't apply to me." This is one of its favorite ploys.

Stalking vs. Indulging

Sharing: I am finding that I feel happy one minute, frustrated five minutes later, and then frantic the next. I am amazed at how crazy I behave when I observe myself.

Response: You are doing well in just stalking observing, witnessing, noting.

Maintaining this stance starts to free us from our emotional charges. There is a fine line between experiencing our emotions, and what the Toltecs call indulging in our emotions.

We can experience our emotions while maintaining the stalking stance. If, however, we drop into depression or selfpity and lose the stalking stance of just witnessing and observing, while not becoming, we are indulging.

This is not easy, and we will all indulge, particularly as we are beginning in our stalking. So, do not beat yourself up if you find yourself indulging (the parasite loves to beat us up). Just be with the emotion (don't suppress it), but do not act on it.

This Door To God

Question: I realize the Parasite's doing a number on me with this one... so I could use some further guidance.

There's some feeling of needing the right book, understanding how to work with the columns, how often to write, the form the writing "should" take, etc.

Ya know what I mean?

As a writer... there's more to writing than "just write it down" because I'm so aware that everything is perception... even the act of writing something simple is an act of interpretation, editing, choosing how to phrase, and so on.

See what I mean? So, I could use some help to get going on the process. And I don't mean... anything to do with explaining its value or anything. It is purely a way to gently clarify the mechanics in such a way that I can begin.

Answer: As a writer, this will be a good exercise for you. The parasite will try to get you to question yourself as to whether you are writing in the Mitote Book the 'right way'. Tell the parasite, "It doesn't matter."

The Mitote Book is only for you, selftoself. You do not need to worry about how what you write is perceived, as you are the only one reading it.

Its purpose is to externalize the parasite. When you recognize the voice of the parasite, write down the exact words it uses. For example, if it is the Judge and it says, "You are procrastinating again: you always do that, you dummy!" then write down those exact words in the left column. Then notice how you as the Victim feel. If the Victim has words, write them down. If it is just a feeling, write down how the Victim feels in the right column.

Remember, this is a stalking exercise. Do not lose the stalking stance. Witness and write down what you observe. Do not try to analyze it. The parasite loves to analyze things. As soon as you analyze you have lost the stalker's stance. The parasite's biggest foothold is in the mental body. When we analyze things, we "think" that we are healing the pattern. Then we forget and repeat the pattern. The parasite tells us that if we can figure it out, we will have grown and progressed on our spiritual path.

Figuring things out is simply motion. It is not movement. When we do the work, versus thinking about the work, we make movement in spite of ourselves. When we *think* about doing the work instead of *doing* the work, we have just fallen into one of the parasite's biggest traps. The parasite convinces us that if we think about the work we are doing the work. We are not.

My teachers would often tell me I was like a dog chasing its tail, much motion and no movement. We can get tired chasing our tail, but ultimately we have not progressed anywhere.

It is like the story about the two doors. One says, "This Way to God." The second door says, "This Way to Understand How to Get to God." The parasite will lead us through the second door.

More Parasite Games

Sharing: I too have been caught in the parasite's games.

The chatter appears to be constant, so I could write in my book all day long.

As I started my Mitote Book and tracked the Judge and Victim, I too was being tricked by the parasite. At first, I thought I was on the right track. Then I realized that I was in the middle of the parasite's game. The parasite is so clever! I was writing down scenarios and rationalizing my reactions and feelings.

Now I know that I should just write what is being said regardless of what it says, and that's it.

Sucked Back Into Old Habits

Question: As I get further into this journey, I am feeling much resistance. It is as if I know where I want to go and how I want to behave, but I catch myself being sucked back into old habits.

I was just wondering if this resistance would be labeled as fear, or is it just that in that particular moment I was not exercising awareness? Or is it the parasite playing games again?

I feel like it is all a game. Then I'll come here, read a post, and have a light bulb moment.

Answer: When the parasite realizes that it is being seen for what it is, it will put up a fight. It fights for its survival. The fight often comes in the form of resistance. The resistance can be feelings of discouragement, despair, and even depression. Alternatively, it can be rationalizations of the mental body making you question what you are doing. One of the favorite footholds of the parasite is making you beat yourself up for not being where and what you want to be.

Keep going back to your deep desires for growth, and retain the stalking stance. Just observe and witness what is going on inside of you your feelings, thoughts, rationalizations, reactions and so on. At this point just observe. Do not try to change what you observe. Do not analyze what you observe. This is how the parasite sucks you in. It makes you *think* you are bettering yourself by trying to change yourself. At this stage, the transformation will begin just with the light of awareness. All you need to do is just stalk yourself. Just continue to watch and observe. Awareness is powerful. The more we engage it, the stronger it becomes.

Just witness, and when you see a pattern or recognize the voice of the Judge or Victim, note it in your Mitote Book. Remember, this is only for you selftoself. There is no one evaluating or judging you. Do not try to change what you see. Let the power of awareness, the intent of this group, and Spirit work for you in your transformation. At this point, your job is just to keep your awareness engaged and stalk yourself.

Wonderful Realization

Sharing: I was near crying because I have come to understand that the parasite has kept me far from me since my birth. The parasite makes me feel that I am not beautiful enough, not clever enough, and not rich enough... And I was sure that it was true, making my life so difficult for me. And people say, "You are always the best, you must be so happy in your life." I was so ashamed to be so sad. It is so difficult that I would like to cry, to wash my bodies, to clean my Tonal. Now, I really understand what that means!

Response: It's a major milestone when we realize how fully the parasite has blocked us off from who we are, how it has limited us, held us in a prison, caused us feelings of not being good enough, and overall pain.

It can be a painful realization, but also a wonderful one. With this realization, we now know we have begun our journey on the Path of Freedom.

Being Special

Sharing: I noticed my parasite about two years ago, and have been working on not judging or complaining for a while. I find that when I look at the world around me and feel equal with all (no better and no worse than anything), the parasite gives way, and inspirations and creativity engulf me.

I find my parasite telling me that I am too selfimportant, that I do not have to practice the exercises because I already know them. But I know that this is the way the parasite is creeping in. I say, "I'm watching you I know what you're doing!" and write it down in my Mitote Book.

Response: The parasite tells us we are special. This is where our selfimportance comes in. We are not special. Whenever we want to feel special, know that it is the parasite.

However, as my nonphysical teachers used to tell me, "In the eyes of Spirit, no one is special. We are all just as important as anyone else. No one is better than anyone else." However, they would also say, "You are not special. However, it is possible for you to be extra ordinary, or extraordinary." This is part of living an impeccable life with elegance. Elegance is the blend of beauty and efficiency of energy.

Just do it

Sharing: The third entry in my Mitote Book was the Judge telling me I shouldn't have started the book, I can't do it right. The Victim told me I'm not ready; I'm inadequate.

I bet something like this happens to most of us. I believe what Kris says: "Just do it".

What Do You "See"?

Question: Yesterday I received the second CD and began listening to it. It said that a child does not make a distinction between itself and its mother, itself and its surroundings. It reminded me of something that I heard some time ago: If you don't become a child again, you will not enter the kingdom. Is "seeing", in some way, the same as being in the kingdom of heaven? Thinking of heaven and "seeing" made me cry. Crying is certainly a result of some activity of the emotional body. Should it be stifled? Why is there crying for no reason? (I'm a bit ashamed to confess that this is my case).

Answer: Do not stifle the urge to cry. It is actually a gateway to a part of Self that contains an innocence you feel you have lost. Opening up your emotional body will help you connect to this aspect of Self, and integrate it into the whole. It is a wonderful thing when this happens.

"Seeing" enables us to perceive the "kingdom of heaven", but we still need to align to what we see so it becomes a reality in our lives. Who influenced your Judge?

As you stalk the Judge and the Victim, notice their voices. Notice the words and phrases they use. When we observe the Judge, we may find the voice it uses is the voice of one of our parents. It could even be a teacher or another authority figure from our childhood. We may find the words and the phrases it uses are the same ones a particular authority figure used when we were growing up.

Much of our personality is "inherited" from those we grew up with. We take on many of the same thinking patterns, ways of reacting, beliefs and so on. The personality is not who we are. In the Mastery of Awareness, we stalk ourselves and get to know our personality. In the Mastery of Transformation, we begin to remove our identity from the personality.

Exercise III - Where Did Your Judge Come From?

We must look at why we judge. When we begin to stalk this, we will find that much of judgment is really a learned behavior.

It is important to diligently stalk the Judge and the Victim in us. Most of us are continually judging ourselves, just as we judge others.

Whether we like it or not, many of the false personality traits we have come from our parents. When we stalk the Judge and the Victim in ourselves, we may find that the inner Judge uses the voice of one of our parents.

Be sure to focus on stalking the attitudes, words and behaviors that belonged to your parents. Stalk yourself to find which judgments, beliefs and sayings you have taken on. In this way, you will become aware of these learned judgments and where they came from.

Book of Life & The Mitote Book

Question: I hear the voices in my head, and I also hear many opinions and thoughts that don't feel like they are my own. They sound like my parents, old soccer coach, and teachers.

In writing these down, can I put these in the same book as my desires?

Answer: It is best that you keep the Mitote Book and the Book of Life separate. The intent of the books is different, and so is their energy.

You are on the right track in just stalking the voices of the Judge and the Victim. Do not analyze them, as the parasite loves to analyze. Just observe, witness and note.

The many Voices of the Judge

Sharing: I'm having a 'great' time with this Judge, especially as I've discovered that it assumes several personalities depending on the message it wants to convey. Sometimes it's my Mom or my Dad, whilst sometimes its 'voice' is that of one of my past school teachers (a particularly opinionfull person).

I notice, mainly when I'm 'correcting' my children, that I even assume the tone and inflection of the person I guess I originally learned the reaction from. I've always been bemused by this, thinking, "My god! You sound just like your Mom!" However, I've never got to thinking, until now, about the need to consider the reality of my assumption about what is and what is not correct behavior.

Sometimes, though, the 'voice' seems to be my own, usually when it's giving me a synthesis of all the identified messages, such as, "You're a failure, you're a fool. You mess everything up, etc." The bloody annoying thing is that I believe all this rubbish about my lack of selfworth. Not for much longer though, for when I've seen this artful trickster out exactly for what it is, then it will be the time to give credit for what's right and true about this life.

Answer: Some schools of knowledge call these subpersonalities valences. Not only can we observe them in ourselves, but also if you are around children you will find them repeating the exact words their parents or teachers use, with the same facial expressions and tone of voice.

What is also significant in our growth is that along with adopting certain personality valences, we adopt the dysfunction of the person we took the valence from.

Kids

Question: Wow! The more I write in my Mitote Book, the more I worry about what judgments I'm putting in my kids. I feel like I shouldn't say this or that to them, but what do I do when I don't want them to fight with each other or pull the dog's tail?

Answer: You are your children's greatest example, particularly when they are young like your kids are.

It does not matter what you say to your children. They will sense where you are at in your life. As you release your agreements and live your life accordingly, they too are much influenced by your transformation.

One thing to keep in mind about children, however, is that they have their own personal task and life mission. There is a purpose to their life, and in this dense timeframe, we are all wounded. Part of our personal task is working out and healing this wounding. We, as parents, are responsible for doing the best we can. However, we cannot prevent our children from working out their own personal tasks.

No Expectations

Sharing: The parasite has been telling me that maybe I am not on the path, since there is no trauma and drama going on with me.

Answer: Remember, we all are working on our own piece of the pie. The parasite will want us to compare our piece with someone else's. If you do not have much emotional stuff up in your life now, do not judge it. Nowhere is it said that if you do not have much emotional stuff, you are not growing.

Just continue to stalk yourself, tune into your connection through your desires to be here on your path.

Part of this work is removing our expectations. If we expect things to be a certain way, it is either a belief or the parasite. At any point in our life and our path, we may be working on an aspect that is different from what we were working on a month ago. We cannot futuretrip, and decide what that aspect is going to be. Trust in your process, and know it is best for you. You, Self, is all that matters on this path.

Lies

Sharing: Kris, Kalyn, or anyone who can help, how did you deal with the overwhelming awareness of the parasite being practically in everything you do? This freaked me out last year, seeing its energy... how it works with dependency, how it works in individuals and between people. Seeing small children being 'infected' makes me angry. It still makes me so sad, knowing it is all within me.

Answer: A question to ask yourself, when you get angry at the lies: *who* is getting angry? When you are frustrated that your growth is not moving fast enough, *who* is frustrated?

Who you are, the Essential Self, does not anger or get frustrated with the condition of humanity and the ego self we all carry.

One way to find the Essential Self is to find what it is not, and pull your identity out of what it is not. It is not frustration, impatience, and anger at one's imperfections. It is not drama and the belief that to make growth happen one must get emotionally charged about it. It is not these things. These things are the realm of the parasite.

When we see the lies, we simply take our identity out of them, without fanfare, drama, or beating ourselves up.

Reclaiming Energy

Question: A couple of days ago I was working in my Mitote Book. I wrote down a voice that told me that I should act like things were O.K., even when I felt uncomfortable. I remember being young and having to smile and "be good" when my parents had family or friends over. Today I was tuning into my bodies in meditation, and my physical body felt sad and ignored. After the meditation, I went to lunch with a friend, and I found my hand shaking each time I smiled, because I felt uncomfortable. Why is the smiling making me shake?

Answer: As a child, when we cannot resolve something mentally we shove it into our emotional body. If it is painful, our emotional body suppresses it into our subconscious in an attempt to get away from the pain. When it is unresolved at an emotional level, it gets pushed down further into density, into our physical body.

As we move our awareness into the subconscious, as we are doing in this course, we begin to uncover what we have suppressed and repressed, layer by layer in the subconscious. You have uncovered an unresolved wound that has manifested as trembling in the physical body.

Notice how you have developed a coping mechanism for the pain you experienced as a child putting a happy face on things.

As you keep peeling off the layers of suppressed wounding and pain in your subconscious, you will free yourself up and begin to regain your personal power. It takes much energy to keep all of the stuff we have suppressed, pushed down in our subconscious, out of our awareness. As we release it, we reclaim the energy we need for our personal growth.

The Voice of the Judge

Question: I notice most of the entries into my Mitote Book are voices of the Judge. Most are in judgment of others at first glance. I realize I've been judging people, sizing them up, if you will, for a long time. I can feel how limiting it is in being open to other people, and that it does block love from coming through. The only thing is that I don't seem to place the voice anywhere in my past, as if I learned how to do this on my own. How should I proceed in eliminating this behavior, or is just a stalking stance all that is required?

Answer: Good observations. When we judge others, we prevent ourselves from seeing what actually is. We see our judgment, but not who the person is. Judgment perverts our perception.

Nevertheless, we all judge. Why do we judge others? The first step in stopping judgment is to understand why we judge. As we continue to stalk our judgment, we increase our awareness of Self. We have much in our subconscious that we have suppressed and repressed. On our growth path, awareness continues to move deeper into our subconscious, bringing what is there into our conscious awareness. We begin to uncover the wounds that motivate us to judge.

Right now, all that is required is the stalking stance. We are freeing up and increasing our muscle of awareness. The more we are aware, the stronger our awareness becomes. Our awareness moves further into our depth, through our subconscious and wounding, and eventually to our core. At our core lies the brilliant diamond of Self who we are.

What is What?

Question: I have a question about the parasite. Any work I'm trying to do, especially writing in the Mitote Book, the parasite is always there. It is hard for me to tell where the true ME is.

Answer: In order to keep things in perspective, remember that the energy is "turned up" right now. This causes the parasite to be more active and more visible. It may seem like the parasite is everywhere.

At this point, just continue to note any "shoulds" or "shouldn'ts", feelings that you don't understand or don't get it; anytime you beat yourself up; if you don't feel good enough, or like you aren't moving fast enough; any doubts that come up. Just write these down in your Mitote Book.

In the beginning, it is difficult to determine what is our "True Self" and what is the parasite or false personality. We have invested much of our lives building up the false personality, which walls off the Essential Self. As you stalk without judgment and shine the light of awareness on the patterns you observe, you will begin to have glimpses of the true you.

The beginning is always difficult, because we do not know what is real and what is not. Just trust in the process and keep your stalking stance. At this point, you do not need to do anything with what you see, just observe and note it.

If you wish to access truer aspects of Self, do the process of following your deep desires, urgings and motivation for personal growth. Focus on these and follow them back to your source.

Writing Down Realizations

Question: As I do this work and stalk myself, I see new things about myself. Where can I write these down in the Mitote Book?

Answer: You can write down realizations you have in your Book of Life. Write down what the parasite says in your Mitote Book.

The Book of Life is something you will want to keep. The Mitote Book is something you will want to throw away, along with the patterns you have externalized in it.

Chapter V - Beliefs

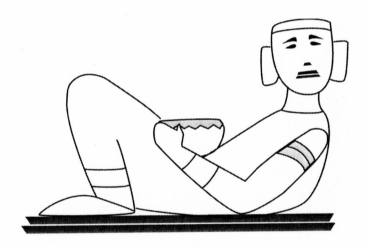

Lesson I -   **Clearing Out Our Inventory**

A fundamental part of the Toltec system of growth is the cleaning out of our inventory. Our inventory consists of our beliefs, concepts, convictions, and knowledge. This post focuses on beliefs. The Toltec body of knowledge, just as any body of knowledge, is a framework we use for our personal growth and evolution. Humans need a framework or system to use in their personal growth. However, in order to experience the Nagual, there reaches a point when we need to let that framework go. We must not turn the framework or system into a belief system.

Belief systems are dense, and pervert our perception. The Nagual don Miguel, author of *The Four Agreements,* would often tell his apprentices: "Don't believe anyone. Don't believe me. Don't believe yourself." When direct knowledge enters mass consciousness, it has a tendency to move further down into density. As it moves into density, the pure knowledge will often be changed. It may become a philosophy or a belief system. Major religions of the world are examples of how original direct knowledge became dogmatic beliefs.

I like to use the following example. When we are constructing a building, we use a structure to climb up the sides, called scaffolding. We need the scaffolding to build the building. The scaffolding is a structure. However, once the building is complete we must take the scaffolding down. The same applies to our growth path. We need a structure or system as we progress on our path. However, eventually we will need to let that structure go. If we turn the structure or system of knowledge into a belief system, it is as though we left the scaffolding up on the building, believing it was part of the building.

Beliefs prevent us from perceiving reality as it is. For example, just a few hundred years ago in the USA, if a woman sneezed too often she could be outcast or even burned at the stake. The belief was that the excessive sneezing was caused by something evil. This is an extreme example. However, we all have beliefs that have nothing to do with what is. When we are unable to perceive what is, we will never be able to perceive and experience the Nagual.

We want to begin to rely more on those things we can directly perceive and experience. For example, most people who are on a personal growth path can perceive and experience their desires for growth. The deep desires and urgings are something real. They are not something we have heard or learned. They well up from inside of us, not outside. When we perceive the Nagual, we do it in the same way. We perceive and experience the sensation of energy of the Nagual. We cannot get to this place from an idea or a belief. As long as our awareness is bound by a belief system, it is impossible to use it to perceive other worlds and dimensions.

Exercise I - Stalking Your Beliefs

Use your Mitote Book to note any beliefs you have. Write the beliefs in the left column. In the right column, note the ways your parasite tries to justify the belief. Note any resistance you have to letting go of the belief. The parasite will resist.

Here are some common beliefs. You can use these to jumpstart yourself in stalking your beliefs. See how many apply to you, and then find other beliefs you may be holding on to.

- I believe there is a reason for everything.
- I believe that I create my reality.
- I believe that what goes around comes around.
- I believe that there are no accidents.
- I believe that thoughts are things.
- I believe that thought forms create my world.
- I believe that Spirit/God will provide for me.
- I believe that sex takes away vital energy needed for spiritual work.
- I believe that if I live a spiritual life Spirit/God will reward me.
- I believe in unconditional love.
- I believe in karma.

- I believe that alternative medicine is better than modern medicine.
- I believe that one should not charge money for spiritual teachings.
- I believe that on some level I am responsible for bad things that happen to me.
- I believe that fliers and parasites exist that feed on my awareness.

Find what other beliefs you have, and write them down.

Lesson II - **Time to Stalk Beliefs**

Personal growth equals change. You cannot grow and evolve without being willing to change. As we speak about stalking beliefs, notice any resistance you have to letting go of your beliefs. Beliefs prevent change. Letting go of beliefs requires change. The parasite fears change and will compel you to hold on to your beliefs. Watch it in action.

Beliefs bind us and hold our assemblage point stuck in one position. Beliefs pervert our perception, stopping us from perceiving the truth of how things are. Beliefs rob our energy. It actually takes a substantial amount of energy to uphold our beliefs.

The parasite will tell you that you need beliefs to function. You do not. Knowing something and believing something are two entirely different things. We know that if we step out in front of a car we will get hurt. We know this from experience, the experience of stepping in the path of things traveling at a high velocity. Maybe the first experience of this was simply a ball someone kicked at us. However, the pain of the ball hitting us gives us experience to base decisions on. Knowing something through experience is very different from believing something. For example, we may "believe" that 20 years from now we will all be in our light bodies, but we have no experience of this to substantiate it (this actually was a common belief about 15 years ago. Many new agers believed that by the year 2000 we would be in our light bodies). As a rule, do not believe anything. Even if you have actually experienced something, take it with a grain of salt. Keep open the possibility that your experience may change in the future.

A master/Nagual does not operate from beliefs. He or she operates from a place of knowingness. When we are connected to this divine place of knowingness, we know what action is the correct action to take in the moment. We know what is right and what is wrong in the moment. This is the place of divine morality, which is fluid. It is not a set of ethics that is solid and stagnant.

Knowingness comes from the plane of the Nagual, and is fluid. As long as we are operating from beliefs, which vibrate dense, we can never reach knowingness. This is another reason why the Toltecs place so much emphasis on eliminating our inventory, part of which is our beliefs. We must free ourselves up, not only to perceive the Nagual, but to be able to raise in frequency enough to experience the Nagual.

We "believe" that beliefs help us. They actually limit us. The Nagual is fluid. Beliefs are stuck in one place.

Being stuck in one place, they make it impossible for us to be in the universal flow of the Nagual. Stalk your beliefs.

Exercise I - A Technique for Breaking Limiting Beliefs

The following is a technique for breaking limiting beliefs. Limiting beliefs bind us and stop us from achieving our unlimited potential. The unlimited aspect of Self is our Nagual aspect. The potential side of Self is our Tonal aspect. Limiting beliefs shrink down our potential, so when essences of the Nagual come through the Tonal they are limited. When we clean, clear and heal the Tonal, we free our potential, enabling us to achieve our Unlimited Potential.

The technique is simple. Not necessarily easy, but simple. We use a powerful function of the mental body to do it – our imagination.

Find a limiting belief. An example of a limiting belief may be that you will never have enough money. Alternatively, another may be that you will never find a loving, healthy relationship. As an example, we will take the money belief. Just sit and focus on your belief. Place your awareness on your belief and let it open to you. Become fully aware of your belief. See how it pervades your life and limits you. Notice all of the areas it is active in. Notice the energy sensation of the belief.

Now, engage your imagination. In the case of money, imagine yourself with all of the money you want. Visualize and picture a new house, a new car, all of the things you would have with your unlimited money. Spend time with this. Notice any resistances or voices that say "no" to your unlimitedness. Move fully into the unlimited abundance. Spend at least 10 minutes imagining with no limits. Twenty minutes is best. Engage your emotional body, and feel what it would be like in your unlimited abundance. Let the feelings come forward. Be with them.

Do this process on a regular basis. Over time you will break any limiting belief you have. Try it.

Beef Belief

Sharing: When I walked in to a restaurant at lunch, I noticed the smell of beef stew (I've been a vegetarian for about 10 years.). It smelled wonderful. I had read on the Nagual forum about breaking routines curiously about food, and how loving the food during preparation makes a difference. I thought I'd try an experiment. Since the beef smelled so good, maybe I'd eat some. My body all but screamed for it when I thought of eating it. I wanted that beef! So, I walked up to the buffet, and got a little bit with the vegetables. I almost started to cry, and felt a little excited about trying it.

When I sat down at the table, the emotion of release made me want to cry some more. I became aware of how I had rejected myself for liking beef. I could feel the hurt.

Believing That I Could Have Enough Money

Sharing: When I started thinking of limiting beliefs, I thought of Kris's example of having enough money. While I do not have all the material things that I desire (such as a house), I feel like I have enough money to buy what I need.

What I feel I want more of in my life is love. I felt happy and energized as I imagined being around loving people all the time. I pictured myself giving hugs in the morning to all my coworkers. I thought of walking into stores and having long conversations with the clerks and patrons.

I created a completely new picture of my relationship with my wife. We talk together and listen without one of us getting pissed off. We'd enjoy each other into the evening, and jump into bed and play some more.

As I created my world of love, the parasite within me would whisper discouraging thoughts. "The world isn't full of loving people. You're not being realistic. Your marriage can never be as full of love as you picture in your head. Perhaps you should leave and start again. People will think that you are weird if you go up and give everyone hugs."

Overall, I liked this exercise. I tried it again today, and daydreamed about having all the time that I wanted to play and travel. Maybe next time I will imagine having all the money, love & time that I could ever want!

Experience or Belief?

Question: As a younger person, I had firm beliefs. I took a stance and protested issues. As I continued to read and learn more, I found some of my beliefs were wrong. I changed. I learned not to take a firm stance on anything and not to believe much... it changes.

I'm struggling with my beliefs as they relate to retirement planning. I have an older friend who lives on Social Security... it isn't easy. Am I confusing experience with beliefs?

I'm now enjoying the stalking... I recognize the Judge and Victim. When I see them, they go away.

Answer: A Toltec warrior is always pragmatic. If it makes sense to do something, such as retirement planning, we do it. It does not need to be overlaid with a belief.

Exercise II - Resistance

Many find much resistance to these lessons. We are attached to our beliefs. One of the reasons for this is that we have a belief that our beliefs are good beliefs. We believe that our beliefs are better than another's beliefs. A belief is a belief. In the contex of our personal growth, new age beliefs are no better or worse than fundamental Christian beliefs, for example. Beliefs stop us from perceiving the Nagual and the total of Who and What we are.

Use your Mitote Book to note the resistance, fear or arguments from the parasite regarding these lessons on beliefs.

Resistance to Looking at My Beliefs

Sharing: Yes, I have resistance! When I was 818 years old, at church we were asked to memorise a series of statements, all of which began with "We believe". It was ingrained in us, we were supposed to agree, and we were supposed to recite it with everyone else. I didn't understand it, I didn't experience it, but I felt that at the time I was SUPPOSED to believe what someone told me I should believe.

I believed that I didn't deserve a family (church said, you must make yourself worthy of a family, and my family was broken, so I thought I wasn't good enough).

Now I believe I will never be good with money.

I believe I will never feel secure or safe.

I believe I will never function well socially.

I believe I will never own a home.

I believe that I won't find ways to finance my education.

I believe that I will never be emotionally mature.

I believed that I would never live my career dream, but I am just embarking on that and it's great, sooo...

I believe I can never be free of my past.

I believe that people won't love me for who I truly am.

I believe that I will always be lonely.

Lesson III -   Does everything happen for a reason?

Remember this belief determines perception, perception determines experience. If someone believes that every time they say the word "damn" something bad will happen to them, it probably will, at least in their experience.

This is the problem with beliefs. They pervert our perception. They cause us to misperceive. Our experience of something is, in great part, determined by our perception.

As for the belief, "everything happens for a reason", the truth is it doesn't. How could it? Until we have progressed substantially in our personal growth, we are controlled by the ego, the parasite, and the false personality. We are cut off from our essence.

The average person lives under the "law of accident." They do not create their reality because "they" is nothing more than their domestication, their false personality.

When we embark on the Mastery of Intent, after we have substantially dismantled the false personality, we then begin our Path of Destiny. We move from the "law of accident" to the Path of Destiny. Our Dreamer begins to cocreate our lives with us and through us. This is when things begin to happen for a reason.

Are there No Accidents?

Question: Can you clarify what you mean by life consists of accidents? If things do not happen for a reason, how can we learn from life?

Answer: Let us look at accidents a little closer. Do you have a hidden belief that things must have a reason for you to learn from them? Accidents are random. If tennis balls are hit to you in a random fashion, do you think you are unable to learn how to hit them back?

The truth is, and if you look around you will see it, in terms of personal growth, the average person does not learn much from life. They have the same problems and patterns in relationships, jobs, money, addictions and so on, which they repeat over and over their entire life.

It does not matter whether things happen for a reason or not. You can learn from a random event, just as well as you can learn from something you believe happened for a reason. If you go by a house and someone randomly shoots at you, you learn quickly to take a different way home. There does not need to be a reason for it.

It is a popular new age belief that "things happen for a reason." Many want to believe this. However, a higher truth is that as you grow and evolve you grow more capable of aligning to the Intent of the Nagual, which does have meaning and purpose.

Exercise I - Excellent Look at the Themes

By laying out your beliefs, you have opened the door to the next step the themes and stories of your life.

Read through your beliefs. Do you see any patterns? Can you spot any themes or stories?

For example, notice how many times you used the word "guilt," and how this theme runs through your beliefs. Notice how the Judge holds up and supports your belief.

An example of a theme would be putting yourself down, not letting yourself enjoy the pleasures of life, putting others first before yourself.

What themes do you see in your life?

On a side note, my nonphysical teachers would often tell me enjoy life! Life is a celebration. You should always celebrate life. When I felt depressed, they would tell me to go play, or go out and buy something I wanted. They would tell me to celebrate when I did something well, to pat myself on the back.

So, celebrate your life! Celebration uncovers the divine child that resides in all of us.

I Believe Thoughts Have Power

Question: I believe in the power of thoughts, be they positive or negative or whatever. I believe that thoughts have the power of gravity, in that once they start they cause their own force and create their own momentum. How do the Toltecs account for the fact that some people have done horrible things and deserve negative thoughts, and others are justified in saying bad things about them? That some people might, in fact, need to hear the negative messages they get from others?

Answer: The Toltec warrior avoids judgments, particularly judging ourselves. In the eyes of Spirit, there is no judgment or condemnation of people. My nonphysical teachers were sometimes asked what happened to Hitler after he died. They would reply, "Nothing."

It is difficult to accept and even to understand, but the belief that "what goes around comes around" does not apply. People are judged and condemned by other humans sometimes (but not always), but we are never judged by Spirit.

In the context of a spiritual growth path, thinking negative thoughts about someone does little to them, but is damaging to us as it hinders our growth. At the least, it is a waste of our precious energy.

Highs

We can have "spiritual" highs. They can be induced by drugs, meditation, or a chemical imbalance in the brain. The problem is that we can't sustain them. We come back down to where we were before. "Highs" can show you the potential, they can cause a shift in the assemblage point, but they do not cause a permanent shift. Sometimes the "highs" can lead to a spiritual awakening. However, we are unable to sustain the awakening. The highs do not lead to growth.

It is only through growth work that we become capable of sustaining a higher platform.

Growth is the work we do in the Masteries of Awareness and Transformation. In the Mastery of Intent, we move from growth to evolution.

Depression

Question: I have battled with depression for many years now, and am taking medication for it. My spiritual friends tell me I should stop taking the drug. I also notice that when I am meditating a lot, the next day the depressions get worse. Should I stop taking the medication?

Answer: Depression is the result of unresolved wounds. It is difficult to overcome because it has become toxic. Being toxic means that we have moved from having a reason for our pain to simply being in pain for no reason. We are just in pain. If we can identify a reason, it can be easier to correct. However, when the depression becomes toxic, we are just in the depressed state. We do not know the reason why.

When wounds are left unresolved in the emotional body, sometimes our psyche, in attempt to rid itself of the pain, pushes it into our physical body. This can manifest as a chemical imbalance in the brain. Once things become physical, they are more difficult to correct. The mental body is less dense than the emotional body. It is easier to change a thought than a feeling or mood. The emotional body is less dense than the physical body. Once a disease becomes physical, it can be difficult to heal.

Psychotropic drugs do not cure the condition, but they can make it manageable. For some, without the medication the depression can be too overwhelming, and no work on Self can be done. Medication is sometimes necessary to help bring one out of depression, at least to the degree where it is manageable and growth work can be done. We cannot judge the need for medication.

You noted that when you do "spiritual" work such as meditation, you move into depression. All that is happening is that you are increasing your awareness, which moves you out of the avoidance and denial of the pain that is already there just under the surface.

The problem is that, whether it is through "spiritual" work or through therapy, the only way out of the depression is through the pain and wounding you have stuffed deep into your subconscious. This will take time and diligence.

We need to get to the point where we can just *be* with the painful emotions without them overwhelming us. In the beginning, this is not easy, as some people have a pressure cooker full of stuff that wants to be released. It is easy to get overwhelmed and fall into depression. We need to try to take a small piece at a time, without letting too much out to overwhelm us.

Find your desires for spirituality. Hang on to this place. Know that you are loved from the inside out.

I am not encouraging anyone to take medication. However, if one has severe depression and is given a prescription by a doctor, there should be no judgments about taking the medication.

Lesson IV - Pill Beliefs

Stick to the facts (as objectively as you can), not beliefs. When you can base your decision on experience, even better. Eventually you will simply know. We do not need a belief to decide whether to take a medication or not.

It does not matter what the belief is. If you have a belief, it will limit you, pervert your perception, and you will not be clear.

My mentor, probably the most spiritually evolved person I know, has Schmidt's Syndrome and Addison's Disease. Over the years, her body's immune system has systematically attacked and eaten away her glandular system. She has no thyroid or adrenal glands left. The list of the steroids, hormones, and other medicine she must take each day is over a page long, more than 30 pills a day. Just one day without meds and she would be dead the next.

Still she has friends, new age healers and the like, who tell her she needs to get off the drugs. They say this out of their new age beliefs. Not out of knowingness. The simple fact is that she has no adrenal glands left in her body. Without the daily supplement of hydrocortisone steroids, normally produced by the adrenal glands, her body would go into shock the first time she ate a meal, and she would die.

Some people have a chemical imbalance in their brain. When we are emotionally wounded over time, the emotional body dumps it into the physical body, and a chemical imbalance results. Once this happens, it can be very difficult to cure. Others have a chemical imbalance due to a genetic cause. There is no cure. There are many people who simply must take medication the rest of their lives, whether it is for a chemical imbalance in the brain, or steroids for the lack of adrenals, and so on.

Many people who are entrenched in new age beliefs say that *we must be natural*, that medicine is "bad". They will tell people who need medication to live a normal life, that what they are doing is wrong. This causes guilt and shame. Many people who must take medication hide it from others for this reason. They listen to the new age beliefs and begin to believe it themselves. When this happens, the belief actually perpetuates a wounding in Self.

One of the saddest things I experienced was a close friend, a woman who was diagnosed with a brain tumor. She and her husband were the perfect "new agers." They were vegetarians, tried to love everybody, and tried to do the right things. When she was diagnosed with a brain tumor, in accordance with her new age beliefs, she thought she had done something wrong in her life.

She spent the remaining 4 months of her life trying to figure out and understand what she had done wrong. She repeatedly said over and over again, "I'm sorry, God. I will do my life right next time."

The truth was that she did nothing wrong. She did not live her life in error as her beliefs led her to believe. Instead of enjoying the little life she had left, she was racked with guilt and emotional pain, all due to her beliefs.

Her last words before slipping into a coma and dying several days later were, "Please forgive me, God, for messing up this life."

Like many things in society, medicine is sometimes abused. It could not be any other way due to the dysfunctional timeframe we live in. Abuse of power, money, medicine, sex, and so on, is the folly of the times. As warriors, we recognize it for what it is, and do not get charged about it. This is part of what Toltecs call controlled folly.

Our focus here is beliefs as they relate to a growth path. If our priority is our path, our quest, our spiritual growth and evolution, we need to look at our beliefs. Often beliefs have an emotional charge behind them. Many times, the emotional charge props up the belief. The belief is merely a cover for the charge.

For example, some have wounds due to a controlling mother or father, their authority figure. As adults, they project this as beliefs and convictions about big government, large corporations, giant drug manufacturers, conspiracy theories and so on.

When looked at objectively, the beliefs and theories they have do not make sense. However, they are blinded by their beliefs, and refuse to see anything that contradicts their belief system.

Beliefs and Wishing to Get Things

Question: I spend five minutes at my altar every evening, and my son comes in and likes to sit with me. Is it ok for him to "use" my altar?

I like him coming to it. He asked me what it was for, and I told him that it is a place where I pray and sit and listen. He joined me, and said that he was going to pray and wish for a new bike. I then talked to him about being happy with what we have instead of wishing to get things.

Answer: You can use your altar any way that you like, including sharing it with your son. Let your altar be an extension of your innerworld externalized.

By the way, there is nothing wrong in praying to "get things." Is there another belief in there?

One of the purposes of an altar is to provide structure for essences of the Nagual to come through to manifest. When essences enter into structure, they can manifest into both intangible (such as love) and tangible things (such as objects).

As we move into the Mastery of Intent, we deal extensively with manifesting essences of the Nagual.

Stalk your beliefs. Do not let them limit you.

Lesson V - Right and Wrong, Fate, Beliefs

In this path, we need to question all of our beliefs. For example, you may have a belief about fate. Most people do not live under the law of fate or destiny. They live under the law of accident. Our destiny comes from who we were before we came in body. Toltecs call this the Dreamer. Until we have done substantial work uncovering who we are, we are simply not in touch with those parts of Self that contain our destiny.

There is a new age belief that "nothing happens by accident." This is true, but it is only true for those who have done enough personal growth to dismantle our thick wall of beliefs, inventory, preconceptions and emotional wounding; to uncover that part of Self that is able to cocreate our lives through us.

True personal growth is the most difficult challenge we will ever undertake. It takes more energy and dedication than anything we will ever do. It takes time and consistency to make movement.

The number of people making movement in their personal growth is a small percentage of humanity. The rest of the world lives in their false self under the control of their parasite. The false self is nothing but folly. It does not matter because it is not real. However, people take themselves so seriously because they believe the folly matters.

On this path, we have a chance for true freedom. However, we must be willing to let go of the folly that binds us. Do not worry about others. As a parent, you do your best for your children, and the best you can do for your children is your own personal growth, with the healing and love that results from that.

The most important person is Self, not the false self, but who you truly are. Whenever you hear a voice that says, "Am I right in doing this?", stop and see if it is coming from a belief. Look at the belief and be willing to let it go. New age beliefs are sometimes more damaging to our growth than traditional religious beliefs, because we "believe" the new age belief is better. A belief is a belief. They all limit your freedom and stop you from experiencing the Nagual.

Lesson VI - Truth and Beliefs

People often ask if anything they believe is true. There are truths, but they change as you grow and evolve. The way not to let a truth become a belief is to remain fluid. Allow for change.

What "truths" are you living by? What belief do you validate because you think they are based in the truth?

Remain aware of what you believe is true. Stalk yourself by observing how you behave based on your beliefs, and what you believe to be true. Chances are that you will find that over time, as you transform so will the truth that you now believe to be true.

Chapter VI - Seeing, Silent Knowledge and Other Goodies

Lesson I -   Seeing and Silent Knowledge

We have been focusing on the parasite. Let us switch for a moment and talk about some of the "goodies" on the Toltec Path.

One of the byproducts of this work is the ability to access what the Toltecs call Silent Knowledge, and the ability to "see." As we move from the Tonal into the Nagual, we move from structured energy to nonstructured energy. Everything in the Tonal and in physicality begins in energy. The Tonal is a condensation of the Nagual. When the energy is given structure, it manifests into form.

Time and space are structured energy. When we move from structure into nonstructured energy, time and space dissipate.

The mental body is the first body of structure in the human Tonal. Concepts, ideas, beliefs and knowledge are structured energy. As we move down in density, the next body of structure is the emotional body. Feelings and emotions have structure and are denser than thoughts. This is why it is easier to change your mind than to change you mood. As we move further yet into density, we have the physical body. If we have a physical habit, such as bad posture, it is even more difficult to change this than it is to change our mood, as the physical body is denser still.

Moving further into density, we move into our outerworld. And denser still, we move into mass consciousness, or the dream of the planet. On the level of the Nagual, there are unstructured essences, such as love. One of our purposes is to provide the structure for Spirit to manifest essences into form. As the essence of love moves first into our mental body, the mental body gives it structure by aligning thoughts and pictures to it. Then we move the essence to our emotional body and align feelings to the essence. Then we align actions of our physical body to the essence. When this is done completely, the essence manifests in our outerworld and our life.

When we have done sufficient work in cleaning, clearing, and healing the Tonal, we are able to move our center of awareness into the Nagual, into nonstructured energy. At this level, there is no time and space. We are able to perceive energy before it becomes manifest, and we are able to perceive the energy behind what is already manifest.

This ability is called "seeing" by the Toltecs, and is related to Silent Knowledge. Silent Knowledge is silent because it is unstructured. There is no noise of the inner dialog of the mental body. To access Silent Knowledge we must rise above the frequency of the mental body, with all of its words, concepts, beliefs and knowledge, because the mental body is structured. Silent Knowledge is higher in frequency. It is unstructured.

To "see" we must break our attachment to our knowledge and beliefs, and let them all go. We must be sufficiently healed of our emotional wounding, as emotional charges vibrate at a level much too dense to rise into nonstructure.

A few years ago, I was talking with Kalyn. She was a schoolteacher at the time. She was talking about a fellow teacher of hers, a woman I had never met. As Kalyn was talking about her, I began to "see" her friend. I saw she was living with a man. Kalyn had never met this man. I "saw" the man had some heavy personal issues. He and Kalyn's coworker had a dysfunctional relationship, and it was harming Kalyn's friend. I told Kalyn what I "saw." She in turn told her friend. When her friend heard this, she become clear as to what was going on in her relationship with the man, and within a month moved out of the man's house and got on with her life.

Seeing is independent of time and space. When working with my apprentices I will sometimes "see" what is going on with their job, relationships, health, personal issues, and so on. This is regardless of whether or not I have met the apprentice face to face (I have had apprentices that live in various countries around the world).

Seeing is a byproduct of this work. When you move up in frequency to the dimension of energy, it begins to develop.

Silent Knowledge is always there at the level of the Nagual. You can always go there for answers. Silent Knowledge comes in the form of what I call *knowingness*. When the mental body gives knowingness structure, knowingness becomes knowledge. When we receive knowingness or Silent Knowledge at the level of the Nagual, it can be like a huge ball of unstructured information. It can take several days for the mental body to unravel knowingness into knowledge.

Seeing and Silent Knowledge come as byproducts to the work of cleaning, clearing, and healing our Tonal. Many try to go directly to Silent Knowledge without doing the work. More times than not they end up in a fantasy world created by the parasite. We are meant to bring the Nagual down into our daily lives. It is the most fulfilling work we can do.

Lesson II -   **Instinct and Gut Feelings**

Each body of the Tonal has its own "extrasensory" capabilities. One of the emotional body's capabilities is intuition. A generalization, but this is why women are often more intuitive than men, because they are often more in touch with their emotional bodies.

The physical body's capability is sometimes called instinct, or a "gut feeling." In Japan they have a word, "haragei." Hara means belly. Some businessmen in Japan are known for their hara gei. They are able to make decisions based more on their gut feeling than the logic of a situation.

Seeing and Silent Knowledge come from yet a different part of the human. They come from unstructured aspects, unstructured realms, above the structured bodies of the Tonal.

Body Intelligence

Question: My wife has been in Florida for two weeks, waiting for her daughter to have a baby any minute now. All last week I had some real intense physical sensations that I can only describe as feeling "antsy" during my daily meditation practice. This morning I figured I'd give it another try, and the feeling was gone. About two thirds of the way through the usual hour of meditation, the phone rang and it was her telling me the baby was being delivered.

Could the sensation have been some form of perception on a higher level of the overwhelm that my wife was feeling, and stopped at the time of birth?

Answer: Each one of the bodies of the Tonal possesses their own intelligence. The physical body, for example, is able to perceive beyond space and time. We sometimes call this a "gut feeling." It is connected to the instinctual nature of the physical body. As we know, animals' instinctual nature can also transcend space and time. This is actually different than intuition, which is more connected to the emotional body.

If through your wife you have emotional and energetic ties to the new mother, your physical body can sense her physical body.

Tuning into the bodies of the Tonal brings us awareness to their innate intelligence.

Seeing and Silent Knowledge

Question: How does one begin to see? Is it a part of insight or a gut feeling? Sometimes I feel like I see why I'm one way or another, and then I feel like it helps me to understand why people are the way they are.

Answer: I will answer the questions in the same order you presented them.

1) Seeing often comes on its own. What we see is many times directed by something larger than ourselves. You can, however, through focusing attention, direct seeing toward a person, situation, and almost anything.

2) Seeing is a specific range of movement of the assemblage point. It is a different range than normal consciousness. As we grow and evolve, the assemblage point becomes more fluid, and the position it rests at changes.

I also perceive it as a rise in frequency. The place the average person holds their center of awareness is in the mental body. The mental body is too structured and too dense to perceive seeing. This is why you can't *think* your way to seeing.

Changing the position of the assemblage point and raising the frequency of our platform is what this work is all about. As we clean, clear and heal the Tonal, it becomes less dense and more fluid.

Seeing is a byproduct of growth and evolution. Many people try to see without doing the work. More times than not they end up in fantasy, meaning that they believe they are seeing, but what they see is no more than a creation of their own mind. If they do by chance access Silent Knowledge, unless they have done the work necessary on the Tonal, their perception of Silent Knowledge will be perverted by their inventory of knowledge, beliefs and wounding.

This being said, however, we can, even in the beginning, develop the sense we use to sense energy. It is a specific sense we all have, and is not difficult to do. When sensing energy we sense its sensation it almost seems like a physical sensation. The only thing that stops us from sensing energy all the time is that we have our awareness trapped in our heads.

3) Seeing does require energy, but it is not the same quality of energy as the energy we use to run the physical body, for example. If I am working with an apprentice for a period of time, say an hour, I do feel spaced out for a time

afterwards. Part of this is because I am focusing my attention at a higher frequency than I normally would in my daily life.

It is not something we need to use sparingly. The trick is to be able to hold a piece of awareness focused at the level of seeing, while at the same time holding a part of awareness at the level of the Tonal. In this way, we can live our daily lives in the 1st attention, with awareness of energy in the 2nd attention In the beginning, I would have to go "there" and then come back "here", go there and come back, go and come back. However, more and more the distinction between there and here seems to disappear.

4) Castaneda said when he "saw" for the first time he got the impression he had been seeing all of his life. It does seem this way. When we are in a state of "seeing" it all seems natural, and the way it should always be. In the beginning, when you come back "down" you cannot always remember what it was like seeing. Seeing requires a movement of the assemblage point. The average man and woman's assemblage point is stuck in a small range. In answer to your question, we are not "seeing" all the time at a subconscious level, as this would require our assemblage point to break its habitual resting place.

5) When I "see" the course, I look primarily at the collective flow of energy that is created by its participants. When an individual shares or asks a question, I may "see" their energy configuration.

The first few months I was under the wings of my nonphysical teachers, they would tell me anything I wanted to know. They had all the answers as, from their vantage point, they could "see" it all. However, one day they began to give me fewer answers. At the time, I kicked and screamed, but I now see why they weaned me off of answers. Growth only occurs through doing the work ourselves. When we are given answers, it satisfies the mind and can make us complacent about doing the work. The parasite tells us that if we know the answers we have grown. We have not. We have only increased our knowledge inventory.

Much of the work a teacher does with a student is energetic. A collective group, like this course group, carries a collective energy through which Spirit is able to work. The energy of Spirit, the teacher and the group stimulate (vibrate) particular areas inside each individual. Patterns, emotional stuck places, are stimulated bringing them to the individual's awareness to be processed. This speeds up the growth process. Working on the energetic level also has the benefit of bypassing the mental body where the parasite is entrenched. The mental body is not always capable of understanding what is going on energetically, and therefore is less likely to get in the way of the process.

Chapter V - Conclusion

My teachers would often say spiritual growth is like digging for water. So often people on a spiritual path try this for a little while loose interest and then try something else. They do not apply the knowledge given consistently enough to receive the gift it contains. If you wish to find water, you must dig a well. If you only dig down a few feet and then go to another spot where you think there could be water and dig a few feet down there, and then find another spot and dig there, chances are you will never find what you are looking for. If you wish to find water, it is better to dig one well deep, than a hundred shallow wells. The same applies to spiritual techniques and processes.

There are laws we must use in the earth-life-system. One of these laws is the law of repetition. We must repeat a process or technique consistently to reap its benefits. Spiritual growth is not a part-time job. To advance on our path we must use constancy and consistency. Reading about a technique is not the same thing as doing it. To many believe that if they could just get enough knowledge, read enough books, get enough answers, then their problems would be solved. Unfortunately, quite the opposite is true. You will only make progress on your path to the extent you apply on a consistent basis the knowledge given here.

Another thing you can do to accelerate your growth is to form a collective group of friends and acquaintances with a common intent for growth and transformation. Your group can work together on the lessons and exercises. In this way, you will experience firsthand the benefit of sharing your experiences in a collective. Energetically you will find your group connecting with other groups with a similar intent and purpose. This is a powerful way of quickening your growth. In the near future, it is Kalyn's and my intent to work with such groups.

This book is only touches the surface of the knowledge available to those who open to it. There is so much more, some of which I will present in future books. However, by diligently applying that which is contained here you will make great movement. You will begin to perceive the world very differently. As you progress on your path, the freedom, empowerment, connection and love that awaits you is beyond what words can describe. It is your ultimate journey.

ABOUT THE AUTHOR

Kristopher first awakened to his spiritual path at the age of 18. He became obsessed with metaphysics and spirituality. Every free moment he had, he was either reading a book or trying different meditative techniques. When he turned 19, he began having outofbody experiences and experienced an array of energetic worlds.

Kristopher attended graduate school in Japan where he studied Cultural Anthropology and linguistics. It was during this time he realized how our perception of reality is conditioned by the culture we were raised in. To perceive and experience different realities requires us to dismantle our conditioning.

While in his thirties Kristopher began an intense sevenyear apprenticeship with a collective of nonphysical entities who referred to themselves as the Counsel of Light. Kristopher says it was the most painful seven years of his life, as well as the most wondrous.

By running intense, high frequency energy through Kristopher the Counsel systematically stripped away his falseself, until all that was left was the Authentic Self. As his inner world was methodically dismantled, his outer world crumbled. At the same time, as each layer was stripped away, Kristopher found and connected to something much larger and infinitely more powerful than his false self. Kristopher connected to higher aspects of Self and ultimately, to what the Toltecs refer to as the Dreamer.

After seven years, the Counsel released Kristopher to his own guidance. It was at this time that his full connection to his Higher Self or Dreamer opened. He connected to his "inner teacher" He gained the ability to access Silent Knowledge at an energy level beyond the structure of space and time.

When Kristopher's inner guidance opened to him, he was given many teachings from ancient Toltec Lineages and the ability to access this Direct Knowledge.

The Toltec path is most commonly known through the late Carlos Castaneda who, in the 70's first wrote about his experiences with the nagual (spiritual master) don Juan Matus in Mexico. More recently other naguals such as don Miguel Ruiz and Theun Mares have brought different aspects of this ancient knowledge to the forefront. However, Toltecs have existed for thousands of years in many different parts of the world.

Kristopher worked together with the nagual don Miguel Ruiz (best selling author of The Four Agreements, for several years and also studied with don Miguel's mother Sarita, a renown Curandera (healer) from Mexico.

Kristopher and his wife Kalyn, who is part Mayan, enjoy traveling, particularly to the sacred sites and Pyramids in Mexico where ancient Toltecs walked.

Kristopher's Teachings

Kristopher teaches us that we have entered a new paradigm in spiritual growth. It is no longer sufficient to raise ourselves up to the spiritual planes, we must now bring the spiritual down manifest into our daily lives. This requires that we are able to rise up into the world of Spirit as well as have enough personal power and clarity to bring the Spiritual back down to our daily lives.

Many in this so called New Age are able to rise up into spirit, but their daily lives are full of lack, suffering, and difficulties in relationships and in life. In the new paradigm that Kristopher describes, we must clean, clear, heal and empower the structured aspects of the human personality to manifest Spirit's intent on all levels of the multidimensional beings that we are.

Kristopher's intent is to bring his students into touch with their higher aspects of Self where love exists without condition, where they find their own inner guidance, and where they are able to access true personal power so as to fully manifest their spiritual side into their daily lives.

FOR MORE INFORMATION

For more spiritually uplifting books, please go to the Lightwurks Publishing site at: http://www.lightwurks.com.

For a limited time, Kristopher will be offering an Online Mastery of Awareness Course to accompany this book. Those who complete the Mastery of Awareness Online course are eligible to join Kristopher's Mastery of Transformation Course while it is still being offered. For more information on the Mastery of Transformation, please go to: http://www.masteryofawareness.com.

This book contains a meditative process to access the three bodies of the Tonal. Kristopher has found that it is possible to bring in energies conducive to deepening through the recorded medium and offers a companion CD containing the process. You may find more information on ordering this CD on the Lightwurks Publishing site at: http://www.lightwurks.com.

Lightwurks Publishing LLC

PO Box 38

Peyton, Colorado 80831

USA

Printed in the United States
19225LVS00005B/148-150